Psychology and Education

There are a number of psychological themes which are key to really understanding education: for example, the internal processes of learners, the nature of learning in culture and the influences on teaching and learning. Written specifically for education studies students, *Psychology and Education* is an accessible text that offers a clear introduction to educational psychology on education studies programmes. It considers the key psychological ideas that will support students' understanding of how different individuals and groups of individuals learn and behave in educational contexts and settings.

Looking at factors that influence learning and attainment, the book discusses themes such as the relationship between cognition and emotion, emotional intelligence and motivation. Throughout, the emphasis is on encouraging the reader to avoid stereotyping, attributions and rigid views of learner ability.

Features include:

- a focus on the most relevant psychological themes
- case studies to exemplify key points
- extended research tasks
- reflection points.

Part of the *Foundations of Education Studies* series, this timely textbook is essential reading for students coming to the study of educational psychology for the first time. It will ensure that undergraduate students are confident and competent with core psychological ideas related to education and help them to understand how different individuals learn and behave in educational contexts and settings.

Diahann Gallard is a senior lecturer at Liverpool John Moores University, UK.

Katherine M. Cartmell is a senior lecturer at Liverpool John Moores University, UK.

Foundations of Education Studies Series

This is a series of books written specifically to support undergraduate education studies students. Each book provides a broad overview to a fundamental area of study exploring the key themes and ideas to show how these relate to education. Accessibly written with chapter objectives, individual and group tasks, case studies and suggestions for further reading, the books will give students an essential understanding of the key disciplines in education studies, forming the foundations for future study.

Philosophy and Education: An introduction to key questions and themes
Joanna Haynes, Ken Gale and Mel Parker

Research and Education
Will Curtis, Mark Murphy and Sam Shields

Policy and Education
Paul Adams

Psychology and Education
Diahann Gallard and Katherine M. Cartmell

Forthcoming titles

Sociology and Education
Richard Waller and Chrissie Rogers

Psychology and Education

Diahann Gallard and
Katherine M. Cartmell

Routledge
Taylor & Francis Group

LONDON AND NEW YORK

First published 2015
by Routledge
2 Park Square, Milton Park, Abingdon, Oxon OX14 4RN

and by Routledge
711 Third Avenue, New York, NY 10017

Routledge is an imprint of the Taylor & Francis Group, an Informa business

British Library Cataloguing in Publication Data
A catalogue record for this book is available from the British Library

Library of Congress Cataloging in Publication Data
Gallard, Diahann.
Psychology and education/Diahann Gallard, Katherine M. Cartmell.
pages cm
(Foundations of education studies)
1. Educational psychology. I. Cartmell, Katherine M. II. Title.
LB1051.G2176 2014
370.15—dc23
2014024747

ISBN: 978-1-138-78348-5 (hbk)
ISBN: 978-1-138-78349-2 (pbk)
ISBN: 978-1-315-76866-3 (ebk)

Typeset in Bembo
by Swales & Willis Ltd, Exeter, Devon, UK

Printed and bound in the United States of America by Publishers Graphics,
LLC on sustainably sourced paper.

Contents

About the authors

Diahann Gallard is a senior lecturer at Liverpool John Moores University. She currently teaches students on the education studies and early childhood studies programmes. She leads modules on contemporary issues in the primary school and learning and teaching in the primary school for education studies students, and she has developed and taught a psychology based module for early childhood studies students, called Differential Development. Diahann's particular area of interest is how psychology can be applied to education and early childhood, both theoretically and practically. Diahann is a chartered psychologist registered with the British Psychological Society (BPS) and a qualified and experienced primary/early registered years teacher.

Katherine M. Cartmell is also a senior lecturer at Liverpool John Moores University. She currently teaches students on the education studies and early childhood studies programmes, where she leads the child development modules across both programmes. Katherine's academic background firmly positions her within the discipline of psychology and this has allowed her to teach across both psychology and education degree courses previously. Her particular area of interest (and passion) is child psychology and how this growing area can be used within education to help children and young people lead happy and successful lives. Katherine holds Graduate Basis for Chartership and is an active committee member of the BPS Psychology of Education section.

Acknowledgements

We would like to express our appreciation to Dr Mark Barrett and Dr Elizabeth Sheldrake for substantially writing Chapter 2. As they are both practising educational psychologists, we see their input to this book as invaluable.

Diahann Gallard would particularly like to thank her family for their support during the book writing process. Diahann's children (Robyn, Evie and Pippa) are a continued inspiration for her work, even though it means that they end up seeing less of her! Diahann would also like to thank her PhD supervisors for their patience over the delay in producing her PhD draft thesis whilst this book was being finalised.

Katherine M. Cartmell would like to thank the students who have spurred her on to write this book (special thanks to Chloe!), as without the very lengthy chats, discussions and emails none of this would have been possible! She would also like to thank her children (Daniel, Kyle, Isabel and Xander) for being such a special part of her life and allowing her to watch in awe, each and every day, how they grow and change in the most amazing ways. Finally, she would like to thank her husband Jay, for being the most humble and inspiring individual she has ever met.

Preface

There are many valid reasons why this book has been written. First, the idea came from our experience of working with the amazing students at Liverpool John Moores University. Having had the pleasure of teaching these students about education, it was apparent that undergraduate students need more literature to support their learning which is focussed specifically on *psychological themes* and *how they apply to education*. Psychology is a basic discipline within education studies, yet it tends to be embedded across different modules, and it is typically **without a space of its own**.

To bring psychological theory into education studies is a challenge in itself because psychological theory centres on precise ideas which students have usually studied intensively as a separate isolated subject, or not at all. Therefore, students studying education are often required to have, or to develop, knowledge of related key ideas from full (and, often, intimidating) psychology textbooks. For example, there are a number of psychological themes which are central to *really understanding education* – about the internal processes of learners, the nature of learning in culture and the influences on teaching and learning, because teachers and pupils are *human beings* – and so it is incredible that more books are not already available which focus on psychology as applied to education studies.

Second, there is a contemporary provocation from within the subject area of education studies. A large number of students now opt to initially study an undergraduate degree in education studies, and then go on to do a one year QTS programme to become a teacher. There are certain psychological ideas which can be said to be valuable for a pre-service teacher to know about; for example, motivation, cognition, emotional intelligence and social constructivism. It makes sense that an undergraduate first degree would be the place to engage with these ideas. Equally, the government is focussed on the quality and importance of teachers and teaching (White Paper, '*The Importance Of Teaching*' 2010) and so if a student gains an understanding of psychology early on it will help to facilitate a depth of understanding of learner behaviour and self-awareness for when, or if, they later become a teacher or any other professional related to education.

One task that educational psychologists have taken on in recent years is to provide support to teachers and educational leaders who have a gap in their knowledge of basic psychology that has arisen from the lack of this input in their training. This is the reason we feel the need to add this book as a contribution alongside the few books currently published and available, as a way to ensure that undergraduate students are confident and competent with core psychological ideas related to education.

This book has been organised as a short, focussed text for introducing education studies students to only the most important psychological themes as applied to their course of study. It will help students understand better how different individuals (and groups of individuals) learn and behave in educational contexts and settings. It aims to provide you with a solid, concise foundation within one book, and prior knowledge is not assumed. Within it are activities and reflection points, plus (as an acknowledgement that this is not a psychology textbook!) signposts to further, deeper self-directed research beyond this book with the provision of the 'Extended research tasks' sections at the end of each chapter.

We hope that you will find this book valuable to your studies, and that it acts as a stimulus for you to go on to develop a deeper, lasting appreciation of psychology.

1

About being 'normal'

The psychological ideas in this chapter
■ the 'normal distribution' measure
■ individual difference
■ normative conformity
■ individual potential
■ resilience.

In this chapter, we explain why it is important to look beyond 'learners' and 'educators' as generalised *'beings',* arguing that we should think of humans more as **'individuals'**. To achieve this, the chapter will first look at some psychological ideas that help to explain the concept of **'normal'**; how it is often used as a way to *judge development or educational attainment,* as part of *socialisation* and how it can lead to *discriminatory attitudes and practices.* There will then be a consideration of the term **'individual difference'** and the ways in which individuals are viewed in educational settings, particularly by teachers. Furthermore, there will be a consideration of the **innate potential** of learners, and the impact that the *environment* and *individual experience* can have on **educational attainment**, and how **personal resilience** relates to outcomes too. Finally, the chapter details some different measures that are typically used to judge the abilities of learners (by teachers and educational psychologists), and the limitations of these measures.

The concept of 'normal'

The word **'normal'** is used in everyday language but it has a specific use in psychology. The use of the term relates to making a judgement about an individual but always *in relation to others*. Therefore, as a concept it is less useful when making a judgement about *one person in isolation*. The term 'normal' creates the alternative state of **'abnormal'**. The term 'abnormal' can be problematic, especially when it is used to describe a person's development or abilities. Think how it would feel if you were to be labelled 'abnormal'! It has a negative undertone, and it is a term that may be interpreted very differently when applied in a non-psychological

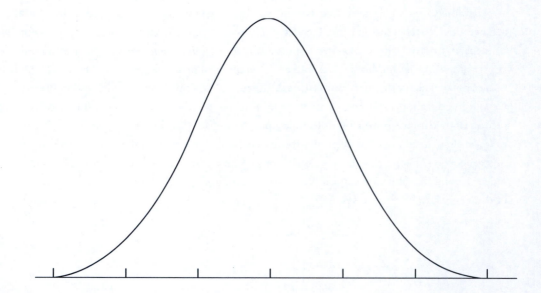

FIGURE 1.1 A bell curve

context. Educational professionals need to recognise that it can be unhelpful and problematic when used in dialogue about learners. Yet, in the right context, in psychology, the terms 'normal' and 'abnormal' are valuable because they act as clear descriptors when measuring learning and behaviour.

To psychologists, **'normal'** is used to explain what is 'typical' (more common or likely) within a group. To fully appreciate what psychologists mean by 'normal' within a group, we should consider the bell curve presented in Figure 1.1 (sometimes referred to as the 'Gaussian bell curve').

What you will see is a standard representation of what is called a **normal distribution**. To explain this, an example is provided below.

CASE EXAMPLE

One hundred people were set a task. They were shown 50 small items laid out on a table for one minute before they were covered up with a tablecloth. The participants were then asked to recall the objects. Each person had the potential to remember between 0–50 items. The majority of participants remembered and named between 15–25 items on the table. Overall, the mean (average) number of items remembered was 20.

Being part of the group in the 'normal range' (termed 'clustering around the mean' or 'within one standard deviation') is seen as 'normal', therefore a score for recalling below 15 or above 25 objects can be viewed, *in psychological terms*, as 'abnormal'. Psychologists calculate a 'standard deviation' to show how far away from the norm (the degree to which there is deviation from normal) a score is. This is a 'normal distribution' measurement.

N.b. *As an introduction for discussion later in the chapter*, if there was only one person taking part, then normal would not exist as there is no one else to compare the scores with!

As outlined in the previous example, the term 'abnormal' is applied as a contrast to 'normal' to explain where an individual may sit within the normal distribution when individuals have been measured as part of a group. It is often replaced with the term **'atypical'**, which is viewed as being *less antagonistic*. In particular, parents of pupils who may not have a background understanding of psychology appear to appreciate the use of the alternative term.

Judging development and attainment

Pupils can be assessed for various skills and abilities to decide whether they are performing or achieving *within the normal range*. For young children, this generally occurs in four developmental domains – cognitive, physical, social and emotional development. It is useful to know if a child is falling outside of what is expected. *In early childhood*, the normal distribution measure is used with developmental **milestones** (markers of 'normal' development against set timeframes) and it allows us to identify when one aspect of a child's development is *atypically advanced* or *delayed* (although identification is really only helpful if it results in developing an action or outcome for the child! *See the section later in this chapter on 'individual potential'*). In *later childhood*, when the child attends school, a normal distribution measure allows teachers and other interested parties (government, local authorities, school leaders) to track educational attainment to gain a perspective on the abilities of the individual in relation to their peers' and to make comparisons within same age children, in the school and nationally.

Views on the value of measuring attainment using a normal distribution measure are mixed. One view is that it is unhelpful to assess children alongside the progress of their peers (because it is unreliable and also may impact on a child's self-esteem). However, others see this type of measure to be fundamental in tracking the progress of the individual so as to identify that a child is not attaining to the expected level in that group, or act quickly when a modification to a pupil's environment or the teaching programme is necessary.

REFLECTION BOX 1.2   Reflection point

Think of a child (you know or have known).
  With this child in mind, make a list of:

A   types of **behaviour** you consider acceptable for this child ('rules' 'expectation') – *the social norm*

B   some **developmental milestones** that you consider acceptable for this child *the developmental norm.*

■   How important is it for a child to be considered 'normal' for behaviour and development?

As part of socialisation

A child's social development is often linked to their **own** view of 'normal'. *As will be discussed more in Chapter 4*, children quickly gain a sense of what 'normal' is through what they pick up from others (within their family, their school setting and in their culture and in society). This could relate to either *behaviour that is viewed as 'normal'*, or to *ways of seeing and interpreting the world which are viewed as 'normal'*. The majority of children will conform to this sense of 'normal' (although for some it will not be an automatic process and they will be driven to challenge it!). The act of changing one's own actions or behaviour towards what is perceived to be 'normal' is called **normative conformity**. In social terms, being 'an individual' is not always perceived to be a good thing. In educational settings, children who conform to 'the norm' tend to follow school codes and rules, and work better as part of a group or community for learning. However, some pupils are driven to express their individuality and actively avoid conforming to **'the norm'**.

Children have unique development pathways and patterns of behaviour and learning, which begin with their genetic inheritance (from their parents), but which also develop as a response to their personal experiences and nurturing (by family or teacher). Although some children may display characteristics very closely aligned to 'the norm' very early in life, other children show significant difference in how they think and act. Some educators do not value children who are 'different' and they strive to ensure that the child is **shaped** to become more like their peers (normative conformity is part of their teacher pedagogy).

REFLECTION BOX 1.3   Reflection point

Think about a child who is 'quirky' (different) to their peers.
  Does this difference relate to:

- social skills or emotional needs?
- educational attainment?
- style of learning?
- behaviour?

(continued)

(continued)

Now, think about the following:

- Does it matter which of these categories the difference relates to?
- At what point does a difference become something that a teacher should address?
- Should a teacher only intervene to address a difference when educational progress or attainment is hindered in some way?
- Does a teacher need to focus on difference when the difference means that the child is more able in one domain than their peers, or they have accelerated learning?

Some children make a conscious attempt to be different, to stand out, which has roots in their sense of self-concept and sociability (*see Chapters 6 and 7*). **Intentional non-conformists** can often be more creative individuals. This is sometimes referred to as **'creative maladjustment'** (as outlined first in Dr Martin Luther King's speech in 1963 as a positive and important thing), although this is more about people being rebellious with their creative and alternative thinking. Those children in the classroom who *'think outside of the box'* can be held in high esteem (as a valuable asset to the classroom and to society), but this, again, depends on the teacher's perspective.

Creative, alternative or 'out of the box' thinking is important, as children who think *differently and creatively* are likely to be better prepared and equipped for the future (Florida 2014). The teaching of children to embrace difference and be more creative in their thinking should, according to Robinson (2011), take greater prominence in schools. But how the teacher views alternative thinking and behaviour depends on whether they are comfortable working with children who do not conform – not all teachers are!

Discriminatory attitudes and practices

Being a pupil who is different can be **'problematized'** (regarded as a problem requiring a solution) by the educator who does not understand the nature of the difference. Clearly, a child who is choosing to be oppositional will need their teacher to explain the need for conformity as being valuable for the wider needs of the learning community. But when the difference is not impacting on others, does this difference need to be challenged? Tolerance is at the centre of this topic. Humans sometimes feel threatened by those who are different to them. This is known in psychology as prejudice. It forms the basis of discriminatory practice, where rules and criteria are created (knowingly, or unconsciously) to reduce perceived difference, perhaps then excluding those who do not fit within the established criteria or follow the rules set. Yet, diverse ways of thinking and acting can be a positive aide to progress and advancement in learning. Children who are allowed to have differences in thinking and views become less threatened by those who are different to themselves over time, and they tend to integrate a wider range of perspectives and form a more open, tolerant mind. Thus, it is vitally important (especially in a child's formative years) that teachers ensure that differences are allowed and tolerated, thereby acting as a role model, so that intolerance and ignorance is not allowed to become entrenched in their pupils' views, and set for their adult life.

Individual difference

So far in this chapter we have looked at some ideas associated with being 'normal' and what it means to be 'different'. It is important to consider more, here, what happens when we make generalisations about learners and teachers or educators. Throughout this book, there will be terms that are used to describe children and adults in the context of education and there will be times when the terms 'learner' and 'teacher' are applied in a general way. We do this only to simplify the prose in this book when explaining particular ideas. In talking about *'a learner'*, we recognise that there is potential to perpetuate a stereotype (a generalised view) which could lead those reading this book to assume that learner behaviour is *rigid* and that, perhaps, *all learners think and behave in the same way*. Therefore, it is important to make this point here to address this. Similarly, when we consider a 'teacher' or 'educator', the assumption is that the *teaching approach* is static and prescribed (through a standard qualification and training). The reality is that all learners, and those who support learners, are ***individuals***. They bring to the learning situation a set of personal experiences and attitudes, and individual ways of thinking and behaving.

Educators, in particular, often have responsibility for a group of learners (rather than 1:1) if they are in the role of class teacher, and they need to ensure that they keep at the forefront of their mind that each learner is an individual, with the potential to vary significantly in how they learn and what motivates them. It may be easy for them to fall into the trap of setting learning tasks and activities for their pupils based on their expectations for the 'typical' learner (the 'norm' within that particular cohort of learners), whereas it has been suggested by Alexander *et al.* (2009) that effective practice centres more on identifying the needs of individuals as best a teacher can, considering the context, time constraints and resources they have. Unfortunately, due to the current focus on standard assessments (Standard Achievement Tests [SATs]) and the process for evaluation of school effectiveness (by OFSTED), educators may need to be reminded of the importance and wider benefits of having classes which contain variation in ability and skills (as is evident across the population and in everyday life).

About 'potential'

When children are born, they are already different to each other, due to their genetic makeup and the environmental influences in the pre-natal period while the baby is developing in the womb of the mother. It has been argued by some that at the time of birth a child will already have an innate and unique way of thinking and responding to the world, even if a fuller personality or learning style is yet to develop. Therefore, children are already on an independent life pathway or trajectory *from conception*.

Today, most educators are aware of the impact of enrichment, or deprivation, that can lead to children not making the educational or developmental gains that they are capable of. It was the United Nations Convention on the Rights of the Child report (UNCRC 1992) which was influential in promoting that children have 'the right' to have access to appropriate environments (at home or in school), with support from the key adults in their lives and from society.

We use the term 'individual potential' to recognise that it is unlikely that all children will reach the same developmental goal or attain educationally to the same level because of the vast differences set within a child's DNA and the infinite alternatives of experience that occur in their life. Therefore, teachers should focus more on reducing any barriers to an individual reaching their potential. In fact, educators must look to enable the potential of every individual, and set them unique goals, although these may be in conflict with some current practices of externally set goals, for example, the National Curriculum attainment targets and SATs.

REFLECTION BOX 1.4   Reflection point

■ Have you ever struggled to learn something new?

  Was it due to :

  o   the method of instruction (how you were being taught)?
  o   a particular weakness that you know you have – for example, in co-ordination difficulty, attention or memory?

■ What did you do about it?

Resilience

Some children are faced with challenging events in their lives, but other children have a (relatively) more straightforward early life. For example, children who have grown up in situations where there is absolute poverty, social problems or abusive relationships, have been found to have significantly decreased life chances and may go on to have social or emotional maladjustment in their adult life (Field 2010). However, there are children who have experienced adversity in their childhood but who still attain well by the end of their schooling, who are emotionally secure or socially competent and who have reached their 'individual potential'. It has been proposed that the source of this success relates to **intrinsic motivation** (an internal driver of behaviour that pushes an individual towards achieving their potential). This is an innate and protective factor that enables an individual to deal with change, which psychologists call **resilience**. Resilience has been found to allow children to reach the goals that teachers set, but, perhaps even more importantly, the goals they set for themselves.

Identifying 'potential' and 'difference' in learners

In order for a teacher to gain a perspective on what a learner can do well, and what they are less competent with, there needs to be an **assessment** made. Teachers may set tests or make observations at the start of working with a particular pupil or class, so that there is a point of reference to later judge progress and consider how learning or behaviour has changed over time. Initial assessment results are called the **baseline**. They are *formative* assessments using tests and/or observations (because they provide information and awareness for teachers to plan for effective, personalised learning) and often they relate to a specific subject or skill within the curriculum, although they can also relate to other areas such as sociability or behaviour. Formative assessment may then be repeated and, eventually, an overall profile emerges, allowing some comparisons and judgements to be made against earlier tests and observations. These are *summative* assessments (because they provide information and awareness following teacher input). If a child is not making sufficient progress in relation to the prior targets set or expected levels, then teachers (and those monitoring progress in a school) will begin to consider whether

- the teaching strategies need further modification
- the child has a specific need that requires support.

The teacher then will be expected to modify their teaching strategies. However, if the child has a specific difficulty then specialist teaching or behaviour support (financed internally, or provided by Local Authority specialist groups) may be accessed. Learning mentors are employed in some settings to provide collaborative support (for both teachers and families) and also to work with children who may have a learning difficulty that would benefit from 1:1

support (for things like self-organisation and strategies for learning or pastoral support where life events may impact on learning or behaviour).

Tools used by educational psychologists

An educational psychologist may be employed (through the school or privately) to help uncover any potential needs of a child; for example, when the child's abilities require some form of differentiation, or when a difficulty is global (across different domains or subject areas). The work of the educational psychologist is varied, but primarily it involves liaising with parents, teachers and the child to unpick prior judgements made by the parents or educators and to measure progress and achievement in an unbiased and impartial way. *If you would like to find out more about the role of the educational psychologist, then see the links and related literature signposted in the 'Extended Research Tasks' section at the end of this chapter.*

Educational psychologists utilise a wider range of tools and instruments, but the most frequently used is the British Ability Scales (provided by a company called GL Assessment – *a link to their webpage is provided at the end of this chapter*). The British Ability Scales are a tool to assess knowledge, thinking and cognitive skills of children from pre-school age to the end of compulsory schooling. At the time of writing, the third edition (BAS3) is the most up-to-date version of the British Ability Scales. The BAS3 has three **'achievement scales'**: *number skills, spelling* and *word reading*. There are also **'cognitive scales'** that measure mental abilities which are significant for learning and educational performance. These include a **General Conceptual Ability** (GCA) score which is sub-classified into *verbal ability, non-verbal reasoning ability* and *spatial ability*. There are also **'diagnostic scales'** that measure a range of specific cognitive abilities. The batteries of tests are stated by GL Assessment to 'enable the evaluation of discrepancies between school achievement and cognitive ability' (GL Assessment 2014), which helps to identify which abilities and/or difficulties are likely to be a result of the teaching environment. The main benefit of using a standard instrument like the BAS3 is that it takes away the potential for bias (a tendency to make a judgement based on prior assumptions and personal viewpoints of teachers). Furthermore, it provides an additional level of confidence that results are a true reflection of a learner at a specific point in time because the measurement tool has been repeatedly *tested to be reliable* (research has been conducted into how effective it is). However, the BAS3 is just one example of a validated measure that an educational psychologist may use. However, we must still remain cautious of any instrument used, as there will remain the associated problems stemming from how the battery of tests is *conducted*. For example, when a test is carried out it is usually as a snapshot opportunity – would the outcome have been different on a different day, at a different time? With an unfamiliar adult, would the same score have occured if the person overseeing the testing was *more familiar to the child*? Would there have been a difference if the child had or had not *taken a liking to the adult*? Often, the testing occurs outside of the home or classroom, in a neutral space (an empty classroom or the psychologist's office) and so *not being in their usual environm*ent may have an impact on how the child performs.

It is important to be aware that there are many instruments that have been acknowledged as reliable only because they have been tested to be so by the author/publisher themselves. These tools are indicative and helpful as a tool but they should not be considered in isolation, and should never replace judgements made by those adults who have an ongoing, close relationship with the child.

Identification of difference

> **REFLECTION BOX 1.5   Reflection point**
>
> ■ Do you differentiate between a 'learning disability', 'additional educational need' and 'alternative educational need'?
>
> ■ Can you think of an example for each one?

When children fall outside of the 'norm' in education, due to **learning difficulties** or **learning strengths**, specific attention to the needs of the individual may be required. For significant learning needs, an Education, Health and Care Plan can be requested which facilitates the *statutory requirement for modification for a child* based on their specific needs.

A **learning disability** tends to be a permanent impairment with a particular limit set on individual potential for a particular cognitive process, whereas a **specific learning difficulty** may be something that can be addressed with specialist support. Although a cognitive or developmental delay identified in early childhood can be indicative that learning potential may be limited, there is still a possibility that they will achieve well in the future. The identification of their **learning need** gives a valuable insight to adults involved with the child, but we should remember that identified needs also relate to *very able children* who are 'above the norm', and they may need support and differentiated activities too!

Some children struggle with the general teaching methods and activities that are provided by their teacher, and for them an alternative programme may be more suitable. The programme can be within the **mainstream setting** or an alternative one, but this will depend entirely on the particular child; their needs and their situation. There is a wider view that alternative systems of education, like *Steiner-Waldorf* or *Summerhill School*, have different pedagogies and practices that may be more suitable for particular temperaments and learning styles because they match the learning needs of some child more closely. *If you would like to learn more about these examples (Steiner-Waldorf or Summerhill School), see the links and related literature signposted in the 'Extended Research Tasks' section at the end of this chapter.*

Throughout this chapter there have been regular references to **'normal'**, **'the norm'** and **'potential'**. Hopefully, the explanations will have given you a deeper understanding of individual difference and, therefore, prepared you to engage with the themes that will be discussed in the chapters to come. The main idea in this chapter is that *learners are individuals*. In applying the idea of 'individuality' to the study of education, we must recognise how to frame it. The message, for anyone who is interested in applying the ideas from this chapter in a practical educational context, is that the terms 'typical' and 'atypical' should be better understood when working in an educational setting. The practical recommendation that comes from this chapter is that, although the terms 'normal' and 'abnormal' can be transferred to education practice, this should happen only when applied specifically as a psychological idea.

EXTENDED RESEARCH TASKS

To learn more about the 'bell curve' and its use in psychology, read this article:

- Fendler, L. and Muzaffar, I. (2008). The History of the Bell Curve: Sorting and the Idea of Normal. *Educational Theory*, **58** (1), 63–82. DOI: 10.1111/j.1741-5446.2007.0276.x.

The role of the educational psychologist has been changing in response to contemporary demands. To find out more, read:

- Department for Education (2011). *Developing Sustainable Arrangements for the Initial Training of Educational Psychologists (Final Report)*. London: DfE. Available online at www.education.gov.uk/nctl/careeropportunities/b00201184/educational-psychology (accessed 22 March 2014).

For more information about the British Ability Scale (in particular, the BAS3) tool used by educational psychologists, visit:

- www.gl-assessment.co.uk/products/bas3 (accessed 22 March 2014).

This article explains the Steiner-Waldorf approach and how it looks in practice:

- Oberski, I. (2006). Learning to Think in Steiner-Waldorf Schools. *Journal of Cognitive Education and Psychology*, **5** (3), 336–349. DOI: 10.1891/194589506787382431.

More information about Summerhill School can be found in this article:

- Ovenden-Hope, T. (2013) Rethinking Secondary Education: A Human-Centred Approach. *Journal of Education for Teaching: International Research and Pedagogy*, **39** (3), 348–350. DOI: 10.1080/02607476.2013.796734.

References

Alexander, R., Armstrong, M., Flutter, J., Hargreaves, L., Harrison, D., Harlen, W., Hartley-Brewer, E., Kershner, R., MacBeath, J., Mayall, B., Northern, S., Pugh, G., Richards, C. and Utting, D. (Eds) (2009). *Children, Their World, Their Education: Final Report and Recommendations of the Cambridge Primary Review*. London: Routledge.

Field, F. (2010). *The Foundation Years: Preventing Poor Children Becoming Poor Adults* (Independent Review On Poverty And Life Chances). London: Cabinet Office.

Florida, R. (2014). *Rise of the Creative Class* (3rd Edition). New York: Basic Books.

GL Assessments (2014). *How is BAS3 Organised*. Available online at www.gl-assessment.co.uk/products/british-ability-scales-third-edition/how-bas3-organised (accessed 1 March 2014).

King, M. L. (1963). *I Have a Dream*. Speech given on 28 July 1963 in United States: Washington, D.C. during the 'March on Washington'.

Robinson, K. (2011). *Out of Our Minds: Learning to Be Creative* (2nd Edition). Chichester: Capstone Publishing Limited.

United Nations Convention on the Rights of the Child (UNCRC). (1992). Adopted by the UN General Assembly 20 November 1989 (ratified by the United Kingdom on 16 December 1991).

2

Brain-based studies and individual differences in learners

The psychological ideas in this chapter

- ■ the brain as an information-processing organ

- ■ explanations of AD/HD, Autism and Dyslexia

- ■ learning styles

- ■ neuromyths.

In the film *Sleeper*, Woody Allen's character, Miles, is warned by doctors that his brain may be electronically simplified. He famously responds: '*My brain: it's my second favourite organ*'. What Miles may actually have been referring to was a specific area of his mid-brain, which neuroscientists (scientists who study the brain) refer to as the Orbital Frontal Cortex. This is the part of the brain associated with making you feel good, for example, when you eat your favourite food, enjoy the company of others and achieve or learn something new. This may or may not have been useful information for Miles; he had been transported into the distant future and discovered that he owed $200 in rent arrears. For us, however, brain-based studies, or 'neuroscience', clearly appear to suggest that the study of the brain can help us to develop understanding of how we think, what we feel, what we do and how we all learn. A major Office for Economic Co-operation and Development (OECD) study, *Understanding the*

Brain: The Birth of a Learning Science (OECD 2007), begins to provide research evidence for this. Among key findings were two clear pointers: first, brain studies may have considerable untapped and under-researched potential in promoting effective learning and, second, an overly scientific approach may not be helpful.

REFLECTION BOX 2.1   Reflection point

Consider the following:

'It is better to take pleasure in a rose than put its roots under a microscope.'

Wilde (1998: 55)

'Of physiology from top to toe I sing/Not physiognomy alone nor brain alone is worthy for the Muse, I say the Form complete is worthier far . . . '

Walt Whitman (1885) *Leaves of Grass*, in Asselineau (1999: 347)

In the above quotations the poets remind us that something profound could be missed through an *overly-focussed* study of the brain. It would, therefore, be helpful to think of brain-based studies broadly, in context and in relation to the topics featured in other chapters in this book. A second point to note is that it may well be better to think of learning (which is the focus of this chapter) across the *whole of life*, rather than as being limited to childhood learning alone. This approach should help us better understand any perceived differences observed in how people learn. This chapter attempts to answer two questions:

- What is the evidence for 'brain studies' as a contribution to understanding the similarities and differences for the ways in which individuals appear to learn?
- What could be its contribution to the educational process?

The first part of the chapter considers what is meant by brain studies; its limitations and contributions to understanding emotions and regulation – both crucial in learning. We also consider ways in which this might help us understand different and atypical neurodevelopmental profiles. Here we present profiles such as Autism, attention and focusing issues and academic processes such as reading and numeracy. The second half of the chapter considers what impact this understanding could have on the way teaching and learning are delivered.

What is meant by brain-based studies?

The term 'brain-based studies' refers to a range of disciplines that help to develop an understanding of the physical make-up of the brain, how it seems to work and what it does for individuals. In this respect, learning is one of the most important functions the brain provides for individuals.

Neuroscience is generally accepted as the generic term for what we refer to here as 'brain studies'. Researchers, such as Bermudez (2010), suggest that neuroscience itself is made up of two separate but related disciplines. These are: cognitive science and cognitive psychology. By cognitive science we are referring to the study of thinking, information-processing and learning processes. By cognitive psychology we are referring to what the brain actually does in the real world; effectively, the working of our mind. In this chapter we will also argue that social psychology (for example, Bruner 1990), educational psychology (British Psychological Society 2008) and clinical psychology (Eysenck 2004) could also be included as contributory disciplines. These disciplines are concerned with environmental and contextual issues and are crucial in understanding how minds function in the world at large.

Braisby and Gellatly (2005) suggest that neuroscience provides a broad framework and a range of perspectives that can help develop an understanding of the natural phenomena of the human mind. This can appear complex and, at times, it will require further sub-division. These sub-divisions are:

- biology – the study of the physical make up of our bodies
- neuroanatomy – the physical structure of the brain
- neurochemistry – the chemical reactions that occur when our brain is working and which make the brain work.

Further constituent disciplines of cognitive science include: computer science (digital information-processing), linguistics (the study of language) and philosophy (the study of knowledge). Importantly, Bermudez (2010) and Eysenck (2004) regard cognitive psychology as a linking discipline which helps the understanding of what the brain and mind actually does in the real world. Learning is clearly a key element of this.

REFLECTION BOX 2.2   Reflection point

In your own words, define *neuroscience, cognitive science* and *cognitive psychology*.

- What are the key features of each of these disciplines?

- What might be the reasons for considering social psychology and educational and clinical psychology as aligned disciplines?

- In what way can this theoretical framework support our understanding and practice when helping children and young people learn?

Now try something a bit different. Focus attention on your breathing. Don't exaggerate your breathing but notice the rise and fall in your stomach area as you breathe in and out. Push out of your mind distractors, such as sounds. What seems to happen to your shoulders?
  This is a simple relaxation technique.
  Now think:

- What role is your brain playing in this activity?

Research on brain studies and learning

Research studies suggest that the brain is the mind's biological machinery (Searle 2004) and electronic scans of the brain are now showing the workings of the brain. Research is also providing a detailed and complex picture of the chemistry behind the way the brain actually works. *If you would like to learn more about how the brain works, see the links and related literature signposted in the 'Extended Research Tasks' section at the end of this chapter.* Learning is the outcome of the billions of electrical connections that neurons make with each other in the brain. These form neuronal networks and involve activation between different areas of the brain, and it is the interactions between the regions that appear to be very important (OECD 2007).

So what, then, does this actually mean for learning? We can define learning in many ways but for present purposes it is assumed that it refers to *the acquisition and use of new knowledge and skills*. The OECD study (2007) suggests that neuroscience provides insights that could powerfully influence education. Blakemore and Frith (2005) clearly recognise this but add a note of caution by suggesting that some neuroscientists believe these claims to be premature. There are suggestions that neuroscience provides a scientific-based framework with implications for educational practice (OECD 2007) – a *science of learning*, perhaps?

There are differences between the way neuroscientists and educationalists may view learning. Neuroscientists can be seen as regarding the brain as *an organ that reacts to stimuli*, with neurons and neurochemical reactions producing effects that are then referred to as *perceptual processing* and *integration of information*. Educators, on the other hand, see this as an active process that in turn leads to lasting and measurable specific changes in behaviour. There does appear to be broad agreement and a shared assumption that the brain is fundamentally an **information–processing organ** (see Chapter 3 for more about this). However, the social psychologist Jerome Bruner (1990) gave a seminal warning of the importance of looking at *the impact of social and environmental factors* when considering information-processing models of the way the brain works.

There is increasing evidence to suggest there is a fundamentally important underlying *emotional element to learning* (this is explained more fully in Chapter 4). This may be the result of our historical brain development. In the distant past, this would have had a hugely important effect. Humans still have the same brain anatomy and so have the same responses. Interestingly, the area of the brain that regulates emotions is not fully formed until the third decade of our lives! It is therefore important for educators to understand that brains have stages of maturity and that the learning opportunities we create need to take account of this.

There is a range of what is 'typical' in terms of cognitive development and variation between the ages when children might develop. In terms of what neuroscience tells us about brain development, educators need to know that providing the usual amounts of nurture and stimulation should be enough for children to develop appropriately. Excessive stimulation, especially in the very earliest years may not be necessary, and indeed may even be harmful (OECD 2007). Some people will develop differently as a result of differences in brain anatomy. It is interesting to note that teenagers' brains, for example, are not fully matured and this has been referred to as *high octane, poor steering* (OECD 2007). Again, this has significant implications for the ways in which school curricula are designed.

The stages of human brain development

It is important to draw some general pointers from what the research appears to be suggesting about the stages of brain development. First, there is now some doubt about the strongly pre-determined stages of children's cognitive development (OECD 2007). Instead, it may be more accurate to be thinking not about *critical periods* in which children need to be exposed to for example language, but about *sensitive periods* when the brain is best suited to developing in these ways. Crucially, for educators, there is emerging evidence of the **plasticity** of the brain. This refers to the brain's *ability to adapt and change*. If a period is missed then children may overcome brain development delay to some degree and continue to learn. There are limits to this (see Hannon 2003; Goswami 2005; Rushton and Larkin 2001 for more on the educational implications). To take a powerful, if emotive, example – even the massively neglected babies from Romanian orphanages progressed in all areas once removed from the abusive contexts (Rutter and O'Connor 2004).

The neuroscientific contribution to our understanding of attention, focusing and being cognitively 'available to learn'

Being able to sustain attention, focus and delay automatic responses is generally agreed to be a hugely important pre-requisite for effective learning (Blakemore and Frith 2005). In order to learn we need to **process information**. That means perceiving or taking in the information. Clearly, some people appear to have less flexibility in their ability to learn. This may be a result of the make-up or anatomy of the brain. It is known, for example, that trauma either before or after birth can physically alter the structure of the brain and the way in which the brain functions. But we also need to remind ourselves of the fact that brains can also be re-shaped (OECD 2007).

More recently, researchers have noted that an individual's capacity to filter information and, more importantly, to effectively deal with more than one element at a time (called **'divided attention'**) can vary. Some people can do this better than others and that the ones who are able to sustain attention, and resist conflicting information, are more effective learners. Interestingly, research exploring the difficulties that some people have with attention (if diagnosed this can be referred to as *Attention Deficit/Hyperactivity Disorder*) has found that there are greater delays in the ways that those individuals process several streams of information at the same time (Karatekin 2004). These studies also emphasise the idea of **load** on the processing system as being a key issue. This is important for educators, as steps can be taken in terms of reducing the amount of information that a child or young person needs to deal with at any one time.

Some studies also refer to subtle anomalies in the *frontal lobes* of the brain and *sub-cortical structures* such as the brain stem (Blakemore and Frith 2005). There may be differences in the way neurotransmitters (chemicals in the brain that allow information to pass between neurons) function, such as dopamine, norepinephrine and serotonin. This is beyond the influence of educators; however, designing learning opportunities that reduce load and structure the information given at any one time may enable more efficient control of attention in learners. However, research has also suggested that *physical exercise* is particularly helpful for children and young people with ADD/HD. The research suggests that, compared to control group pupils with diagnosed ADD/HD, those who have greater amounts of physical activity built into their weeks show greater capacity to focus in class (Gapin and Etnier 2001).

Neurodevelopmental conditions

Blakemore and Frith (2005) provide a detailed review of the ways in which brain studies have helped our understanding of Autism. Differences in the ways people relate to others (social relationships and communication) and the flexibility with which some people process information appear to be the generally accepted features of this condition. Now understood as a *spectrum condition* (Wing 1996), there is a huge variation in the abilities of individuals with this particular profile. Many educators will have contact with people with this particular social communication difficulty but not all will have a diagnosis of Autism.

Brain research has offered a number of theories to explain the characteristics of Autism. A leading theory relates to a '*theory of mind*' (Baron–Cohen 1995). This suggests that people with a difficulty in social communication profiles do not have an interest in what other people may be thinking. They may not, in effect, naturally read other people's thoughts in the ways that many other people tend to do. This can have important consequences in schools. It is important that educators understand this as it may help them appreciate the anxieties and associated patterns of behaviour that arise from this. Simply having an awareness of what neuroscience tells us about the features of the condition can help educators to plan and make adjustments accordingly. Seeing the situation 'from the inside out' (Grandin 1995) means seeing the situation from the position of the person with Autism. Understanding what life looks like for a person with this kind of profile can be enormously helpful for educators. *If you would like to learn more about the practical ways of building this into practice, see the links and related literature signposted in the 'Extended Research Tasks' section at the end of this chapter.*

What does neuroscience tell us about ways of helping children develop language, read, write and in numeracy?

Brain studies into **language** are hugely important. Pinker (1997) builds on the idea of humans as being *hard-wired for language*, but needing an environmental stimulation and language rich experience to kick the process into action and for its maintenance. Bruner (1990) and Vygotsky (1986) established the need to reinforce the importance of social factors in the development of language and thought. With this in mind, brain studies have since suggested that there are sensitive periods for language. Grammatical structuring, it would appear, is particularly sensitive to developmental stages, although acquiring vocabulary may not be. For educators, this can mean that young children are equipped to develop both vocabulary and the ways language works (grammar) but that adults, although able to learn words, may find grammar more difficult. Arguably, it may be better to begin second language learning in primary years rather than wait until high school age (Blakemore and Frith 2005). There appear to be particular areas of the brain that deal with language which, if compromised, may be replaced with other areas. Knowing this could be helpful for educators working with learners who have suffered a brain injury.

The importance of a language rich learning context is clear; however, educators might also need to be aware that, for some learners, too much language and too much stimulation in general may not be helpful. Brain studies tell us that there are limits to our capacity to process information. Exceeding those limits can result in unwanted but understandable behaviours (OECD 2007) like a lack of concentration and restlessness.

Language is hard-wired but needs a kick start and maintenance and environmental factors will be part of that process. The plasticity of the brain suggests that, although there are particular areas of the brain that process language (Brocca and Wernicke areas, a part of the frontal cortext), the roles each area plays continues to be refined.

In society, there is a premium value placed on literacy and numeracy, and individuals who have faced barriers to learning are disadvantaged. Can brain studies help in this respect? Brain studies suggest that there may be some subtle differences in brain anatomy for people experiencing greater than usual difficulties in learning to read and write. There is considerable and growing research in this area, specifically in relation to **reading development** and **Dyslexia** (a persisting difficulty in learning to read and spell) and this suggests a mixed and complex picture. It has been suggested that there are subtle differences in brain structure and/or the connections between areas of the brain, but the results are far from conclusive (Blakemore and Frith 2005). The OECD (2007) study concludes that persisting literacy difficulties would best be regarded not as a deficit, but as representing a *different or alternative learning pathway*. People will learn but it will take longer and demand greater application.

Neuroscience also indicates that *phonological* (sounds) and *semantic* (meaning) *processing* take place when reading and spelling, and that targeting both processes may be the most effective teaching strategy. There are also suggestions that, in many individuals, Dyslexia seems to be *phonologically-based*. The neural circuitry underlying literacy is open to change, and are built over time. Literacy is, therefore *not limited to one single pathway*. There are, therefore, many pathways to the '*literate brain*' (OECD 2007: 93). What is clear (and this is of most interest to educators) is that carefully structured programmes that build on areas of a person's learning strength and boost self-confidence and self-efficacy (and are regular and short in duration) can help people adjust and learn the skills required for reading.

A similar picture emerges with regard to **numeracy**. Particular areas of the brain are sometimes identified as being associated with the development of the concept of *quantity* and *number skills*. The skills associated with recognising quantity seemingly become established in the brain early in life (OECD 2007). There may have been an evolutionary advantage to this. However, developing skills of calculation is, like literacy, another *culturally determined* skill. The research also suggests that if barriers are encountered in children learning to carry out mathematical operations, then patient, slow repetition of foundational elements needs to be carried out. Learning *explicit rules* of mathematics requires effort and cognitive flexibility. The brain science in this area continues to develop and further work is needed to explore the educational implications with regard to numeracy.

Why does current education policy appear to largely ignore the suggestions from neuroscience?

There may be many reasons for this; some political, some ideological. There are clear messages to be taken from brain studies that may be helpful for education policy makers. In particular, there is significant and robust research that emphasises the emotional basis for learning (something recognised by Plato many thousands of years ago). This may be inconvenient but it is significant. There are implications from the current dominating rhetoric around raising standards in education (Garratt and Forrester 2012).

The OECD (2007) study places a significant focus on the ethical issues raised by a possible overreliance on a *science of learning*. Much of the brain science is detailed and descriptive. It is not necessarily explanatory and it does not necessarily have a direct connection to what we might do as educators and it is here that social, educational and clinical psychologists may have vital roles to play. They can re-assess and contextualise the theoretical claims suggested from neuroscience, and translate them within the learning and social context. Brain science gives us tantalising insights into the brain, although its application within education studies is only just becoming clear. The next section of this chapter explores the more practical applications of brain science to learners and educators alike. It begins with a re-assessment of several readily available, and often uncritically accepted, concepts used by educators.

Learning styles

I hear and I forget, I see and I remember, I do and I understand.

Confucius

This well-known saying, from approximately 2,500 years ago, is arguably the first documented reference to learning styles. However, it was not until the middle of the twentieth century that the concept of learning styles began to evoke much research from a variety of disciplines. Although the central concept originated from psychology, research has increasingly been emanating from domains such as management and heath care. Now, critics argue, the topic has become 'fragmented and disparate' (Cassidy 2004).

We all have a preferred style of learning, which can be identified by using different measurement tools, but within education VAK theory is possibly the most well-known.

VAK theory

'**VAK theory**' is arguably the most commonly encountered learning styles model used by schools in the UK.

REFLECTION BOX 2.3

Have a go at this learning styles questionnaire.
These questions would be answered with 'agree', 'not sure' or 'disagree'.

- I enjoy discussing my learning with my friends.
- I remember visual details.
- I prefer to do practical activities.
- I remember things more easily if I say them out loud.
- I learn things better if I can see them.
- I want to actually do whatever is being talked about or learned.
- It helps if someone explains something to me.
- I like to use a pen and paper to help me with my learning.
- When I am listening, it helps if I doodle on a piece of paper.
- I sometimes find it difficult to follow written instructions.
- I sometimes find it difficult to follow discussions.
- I like to move around while I am listening or talking.
- I sometimes talk to myself when I'm learning something new.
- I can understand something more easily if there is a diagram to explain it.
- I often use my hands when I talk.
- If I have to memorise something, I might repeat it to myself.
- I like to write down instructions or telephone numbers to help me remember them.
- I like to touch things in order to learn about them.

Now reflect on these questions.

What does this tell you about your learning style?

Current research questions and disputes the reliability and validity of this model, and the notion that an individual's preferred learning style can be reduced to one of three modalities: visual, auditory or kinaesthetic (VAK). This is further trivialised by the idea that a person's learning style can be identified using a self-assessment questionnaire. It could be argued that this is another example of an ongoing desire to classify human behaviour and to neatly provide everyone with a label. Such a 'quick fix' to personalising education is appealing to schools, but can something as complex as cognitive functioning; can preferences really be simplified in this way?

With the ever increasing demand for high academic results, educational research has gone beyond exploring the 'simple' issue of intelligence and has moved towards *motivation* and *academic control*. The notion of a learning style may be an attractive, tangible method of trying to influence academic attainment, illustrated by such assertions. It is crucial that tools, such as VAK questionnaires, are questioned by the educator with reference to their *usefulness, overall reliability* and *validity*. Time should be taken to scratch the surface of the claims being made by such tools, and the *professional judgement of teachers* (gained from their interactions with learners) should be preserved.

The Learning and Skills Research Centre report, *'Should we be Using Learning Styles?'* (Coffield *et al.* 2004), draws on a comprehensive review of literature, and the final report is almost completely dismissive of learning styles theory and instruments. According to Coffield *et al.* (2004): a) Learning styles questionnaires and instruments are not objective measures and frequently rely on the subjective answers of the respondents, b) Many test items are ambiguous, and many popular models are promoted by vested interests and commercialism, and actively avoid academic scrutiny or criticism, c) Prominence is often unjustified because learning styles, however valid, are only one of a host of issues in the complex learning process and d) Conclusions drawn from increasingly elaborate statistical analysis are often increasingly simplistic. The Coffield *et al.* (2004) report is disparaging of the concept of learning styles and argues that the notion can create limiting approaches to teaching and learning, and lead to all teaching strategies aiming to touch on all styles at some point during a lesson.

'I'm a left-brain, she's a right-brain person' – an example of a neuromyth

There are many neuromyths that have developed from some knowledge of research being applied it out of context. The following is an example of such a case.

Neuromyths can develop from research findings. In particular, there was the emergence of the concept of '*left brain thinking*' and '*right brain thinking*', together with the idea of a *dominant hemisphere*. This led to the notion that each individual depends more on one of the two hemispheres, leading to a 'right brained' person being *intuitive and emotional,* and a *rational and analytical person* being characterised as 'left brained'. Creativity, music and art were deemed to be right brain specific and analysis and logic dependent on the left hemisphere. These concepts are clearly scientific misinterpretations as the two halves of the brain cannot be so easily separated. Although the right-brain/left-brain theory is a myth, its popularity persists. Popular psychology in the form of magazine articles, online questionnaires and self-help texts (which claim to help you understand your strengths and weaknesses in certain areas) suggest that you can be helped through this understanding to develop better ways to learn and study. However, if educators opt to use one of the quizzes that are available, they should do so with caution and an awareness of the potential for misrepresentation about the nature of the learner's cognitive abilities and skills.

In the following chapter, the theme of cognition continues and looks at some of the more accepted psychological ideas associated with thinking and learning.

EXTENDED RESEARCH TASKS

An excellent short primer about the brain is available which should help you understand more about how the brain works:

■ O'Shea, M. (2005). *The Brain: A Very Short Introduction (Very Short Introductions Series)*. Oxford: Oxford University Press.

The *Journal of Neuropsychology* is an excellent place to find out more about the most recent neuroscience research. You can access it via the Wiley Online Library:

■ http://onlinelibrary.wiley.com/journal/10.1111/(ISSN)1748-6653 (accessed 22 March 2014).

For an account of Autism, read this article:

- Barrett, M. (2006). 'Like Dynamite Going off in my Ears': Using Autobiographical Accounts of Autism with Teaching Professionals. *Educational Psychology in Practice*, **22** (2), 95–110. DOI: 10.1080/02667360600668170.

To find out more about teaching children with Autism:

- Jordan, R. and Powell, S. (1995*). Understand & Teach Children with Autism*. Chichester: John Wiley & Sons Limited.

References

Asselineau, R. (1999). *The Evolution of Walt Whitman*. Iowa City: The University of Iowa.

Baron-Cohen, S. (1995). *Autism: The Facts*. Oxford: Oxford University Press.

Bermudez, J. L. (2010). *Cognitive Science: An Introduction to the Science of the Mind*. Cambridge: Cambridge University Press.

Blakemore, S. and Frith, U. (2005). *The Learning Brain: Lessons for Education*. London: Blackwell.

Braisby, N. and Gallatly, A. (2005). *Cognitive Psychology*. Oxford: Oxford University Press.

British Psychological Society. (2008). The Development of Literacy: Implications of Current Understanding for Applied Psychologists and Educationalists. *Educational and Child Psychology*, **25** (3).

Bruner, J. (1990). *Acts of Meaning*. Cambridge, MA: Harvard University Press.

Cassidy, S. (2004). Learning Styles: An Overview of Theories, Models, and Measures. *Educational Psychology*, **24** (4), pp. 419–444.

Coffield, F., Moseley, D., Hall, E. and Ecclestone, K. (2004). *Should we Be Using Learning Styles? What Research Has to Say to Practice*. London: Learning & Skills Research Centre.

Eysenck, M. (2004). Applied Clinical Psychology: Implications of Cognitive Psychology for Clinical Psychology and Psychotherapy. *Journal of Clinical Psychology*, **60** (4), pp. 393–404.

Gapin, J. and Etnier, J. L. (2001). The Relationship between Physical Activity and Executive Functioning Performance in Children with Attention Deficit/Hyperactivity Disorder. *Journal of Sport and Exercise Psychology*, **32**, pp. 753–763.

Garratt, D. D. and Forrester, G. (2012). *Education Policy Unravelled*. London: Continuum.

Goswami, U. (2005). The Brain in the Classroom? The State of the Art. *Developmental Science*, **8** (6), pp. 468–469.

Grandin, T. (1995). How People with Autism Think and Learn. In E. Schopler and G. Mesibov (Eds), *Learning and Cognition in Autism*. New York: Plenum Press.

Hannon, P. (2003). Developmental Neuroscience: Implications for Early Childhood Intervention and Education. *Current Paediatrics*, **13**, pp. 58–63.

Karatekin, C. (2004). A Test of the Integrity of the Components of Baddeley's Model of Working Memory in Attention-Deficit/Hyperactivity Disorder (ADHD). *Journal of Child Psychology and Psychiatry*, **45** (5), pp. 912–926.

Organisation for Economic Co-operation and Development (OECD). (2007). *Understanding the Brain: The Birth of a Learning Science*. Centre for Educational Research and Innovation.

Pinker, S. (1997). *How the Mind Works*. London: Penguin.

Rushton, S. and Larkin, E. (2001). Shaping the Learning Environment. Connecting Developmentally Appropriate Practice to Brain Research. *Early Childhood Education Journal*, **29** (1), pp. 25–33.

Rutter, M. and O'Connor, T. (2004). Are there Biological Programming Effects for Psychological Development? Findings from a Study of Romanian Adoptees. *Developmental Psychology*, **40** (1), pp. 81–94.

Searle, J. R. (2004). *Mind: A Brief Introduction*. Oxford: Oxford University Press.

Vygotsky, L. (1986). *Thought and Language*. Cambridge, MA: MIT Press.

Wilde, O. (1998). *Oscar Wilde's Wit and Wisdom: A Book of Quotations*. Mineola, NY: Dover Publications.

Wing, L. (1996). *The Autism Spectrum*. London: Constable.

3

Cognition and metacognition in education settings

The psychological ideas in this chapter
■ the information-processing approach
■ the Working Memory Model
■ cognitive efficiency
■ metacognition
■ Piagetian theory
■ overlearning.

In this chapter we look at **cognition**. Cognition is a term that is often used by teachers and educators, but with a limited understanding of what it actually is. It is important for anyone studying education to be aware of the nature of human cognition, and so, in this chapter, we will present an overview of some of the key ideas associated with cognition that psychologists use, and explain how they can be applied in education studies.

Cognition is about how humans **process information**. It is how people see, interpret, remember and imagine the information that is around them. It is how we, as humans, process information and it relates closely to *how we learn*. Therefore, being aware of the main ideas that psychologists use to explain how humans perceive and engage with the information from their environment enables those involved in education to be more aware of the needs of learners.

REFLECTION BOX 3.1   Understanding yourself first

■ Are you 'quick' to pick up on new information and enjoy fast paced learning? Or do you prefer information to be provided for you at a slower pace?

■ How easily is it for you to remember and recall:
  — numbers?
  — names and places?
  — events (both ordinary and memorable)?

■ Does your ability to take on new information remain stable (stays about the same)? Or does it vary depending on:
  — how you feel?
  — where you are?
  — the time of day, month or year?

The 'information-processing' approach

Psychologists separate out *'direct experience'* (what we see, feel, hear, smell and taste), *'sensation'* (physiological and biological experience managed by the brain) and *'representation'* (imagery and conceptualisation), which, together, explain the fuller **cognitive process**. Humans tend to manage information in *similar ways* and psychologists have created various models of information processing to share and to test ideas, within what is known as the **information-processing approach**. *In this chapter, we provide a succinct overview of this approach but to find out more, see the links and related literature signposted in the 'Extended Research Tasks' section at the end of this chapter.*

The goal of the information-processing approach is to specify which processes underlie cognitive performance (leaner knowledge and behaviour).

The model provided in Figure 3.1 shows the process of how a learner is directly influenced by the *'stimulus'* (the information that is received), how the information is used and what happens next. A product of the process is a *'response'* or *'action'* (sometimes referred to as a **behaviour outcome**). It should be noted, however, that it is possible to also process information *in reverse*, beginning with the *individual's expectations and knowledge*, not by the stimulus itself.

The model in Figure 3.1 is *hypothetical* (imagined, as a tool to aid conceptualisation). Models such as the one provided can be helpful but equally they can misrepresent cognition

Basic model

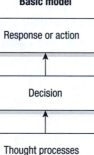

FIGURE 3.1 A basic model of how people tend to process information

as a *serial process* (where we move through one process at a time) when in fact most cognition involves *parallel processing* (various processes occurring in different ways, at different rates and at different points at the same time).

REFLECTION BOX 3.2   Reflection point

Think of how you engage in lectures. One strategy to engage with the information being provided is to *write notes with a pencil or type notes on a device.*

■   Can you map what happens when taking notes (against the basic model provided in Figure 3.1)?

    —   What is the sequence of functions?

    —   What type of processing do you use?

The information-processing approach used by psychologists can be applied in relation to teaching and learning. It is particularly helpful as a way to look beyond learners as *passive recipients* of information. Learning *never* stops; the human brain continually scans for new information. There are very few times when we escape to total isolation, away from all external stimuli. Therefore, learning is a perpetual activity, and children will be learning even when they are in a passive state. Even when children *look and act* disengaged (or, internally, feel demotivated and/or 'bored') a series of 'systems' are occurring so as to make sense of their experience. It may not be disengagement but learning is unrelated to the teacher's aims and objectives!

As discussed in Chapter 1, there are *individual differences* in cognitive processing (the efficiency of our cognitive processes) and various strategies may be used by different individuals, which vary depending on the situation that they are in. Pupils process information in different ways because of the way the information is transformed and interpreted by the brain (how the information is 'perceived') varying for each pupil. Even when the same information is imparted, or an identical experience is provided, there will always be a different value and meaning assigned to it depending on who is 'receiving' it. *You can learn more about this by looking more in depth at literature about philosophical beliefs on the nature of reality, by referring to the links and related literature signposted in the 'Extended Research Tasks' section at the end of this chapter.*

The historical context for the information-processing approach

In the 1950s and 1960s, researchers began to see similarities between human thinking and the new computers that emerged in that era. Allen Newell and Herbert Simon were among the first to suggest that humans and computers could *both* be viewed as 'general symbol manipulators' and that our knowledge of computers could be used as a *metaphor* for exploring human cognition (Newell and Simon 1972). The idea was *not* that humans *are* computers, but that computers could be used as a way of exploring how human cognition 'works' and as *a tool* for expressing ideas about how humans process information. Information-processing studies of cognition increased in popularity in the 1960s and 1970s, and the modelling of cognitive processes has advanced significantly as computers have continued to become increasingly efficient and sophisticated.

Researchers in the field of **Artificial Intelligence (AI)** continue to make comparisons between human thinking and computers, and some psychologists and philosophers remain dedicatedly focussed on equating human learning with the functioning of a computer. There are those who remain resolute that it is only a matter of time before human cognition will be recreated in a robot, with Alan Mathison Turing being the first to hypothesise that human thinking recreated artificially is imminent (Turing 1950). He created his Turing Test prize to reward the first person to do so. Yet, Searle, a philosopher, has led *against* the possibility of *true* AI ever being possible. He proposed that artificial human cognition will always be 'artificial' and so will never have the true feature of consciousness to be considered 'human' (Searle 2004). His argument was that, although computers may appear to converse in natural language, they are not capable of true human cognition; *understanding* language, thought, human consciousness or free will ('the essence of humanity'). Searle (ibid.) proposed that computers *could* attain a state whereby their processes are sophisticated enough to mimic a human but only as *akin* to human cognition. *To learn more about the possibilities around computers attaining a state of cognition to fully mimic a human being, see the links and related literature signposted in the 'Extended Research Tasks' section at the end of this chapter.*

Some key processes in processing information

Psychologists have identified some key processes that people use when processing information:

1 **Perceptual processes** – we 'code' direct experience and sensation (mental tagging) but we can also create 'representations' of what we have coded (a mixing of perception and interpretation) to store.
2 **Memory processes** – we store our representations and also retrieve previously developed representations which are useful for interpreting new information.
3 **Problem–solving and reasoning processes** – our understanding is assisted by the context.

REFLECTION BOX 3.3   Reflection point

■ Can you think of times in your learning when you have been aware of your *perceptual, memory, problem-solving* and *reasoning* processes?

■ Do you feel that you use, or are aware of, one particular process more than the others?

CASE EXAMPLE 3.1   Look at this photograph

© Diahann Gallard

You may well be looking at this photograph for the first time.

■   Can you give an overall summary of what this photograph is of and what is happening?

■   What experiences do you have of this context and how is that informing your understanding of what is happening?

Now cover up the photo.

■ What can you remember about the photograph? What are the important features?

Now look again.

■ Which features were the first to be recalled? Why those features?

■ Which cognitive processes did you employ?

   — perception?
   — memory?
   — problem-solving?
   — reasoning?

How do we identify cognitive processes in learners?

Researchers who use the information-processing approach to understanding learning focus *less* on whether or not children solve problems correctly, and *more* on **how** problems are solved and the speed with which they do it. It was Vernon (1987) who suggested that faster reaction times correlate to a higher IQ (with a gap between individuals becoming apparent soon after birth). The idea is that **faster processing speed** enables **better performance** on particular cognitive tasks (think in terms of the cogs of a machine, built well, oiled well and working efficiently at great speed!) for example, in reading (Leather and Henry 1994; Gathercole *et al.* 2006) and mathematics (McLean and Hitch 1999; Swanson and Beebe-Frankenberger 2004; Geary 2005; Passolunghi *et al.* 2007).

The *strategies* of competent learners who achieve well are also the focus of study by psychologists, in the hope that clues can be uncovered so as to enable *all* children to be helped towards '**cognitive efficiency**'. In reality, these studies are limited to what works well for *the individuals being studied* and it is difficult to apply and generalise the findings as a rule for all learners. A pragmatic view on research into cognitive strategies is that *listening to children talk* about their particular strategies (by asking appropriate questions at the appropriate times) is the best way to understand the individual learner and address their particular learning needs. This is a general teaching approach that many teachers use to find out how individual children think, and to ascertain the pupil's understanding of new concepts and ideas (for example, in the working out of a sum or the plan for story development). As most teachers would acknowledge, uncovering the precise thinking strategies of pupils is difficult, which is also acknowledged in Black and Wiliam's idea of the learner being a 'Black Box' (Black and Wiliam 1990). Children need a wide vocabulary, syntax and self-awareness to be even begin to fully explain what they know and understand.

Children are not always comfortable or confident in declaring *what* they know and *how* they know it. Knowing what you know, and how you have come to know it, is called **'metacognition'** and it will be discussed in more detail later in this chapter.

So far in this chapter, the processing of information has been explained as how a learner is directly influenced by the 'stimulus' information. However, there are various components that relate specifically to learning and attainment and the ways in which information is typically *received, retained and retrieved*, and being aware of these components makes it easier to understand the learning process.

Cognitive architecture

Psychologists use the term **cognitive architecture** to refer to the structural characteristics of cognition, which centres on **memory**. Once a learner registers information (as described earlier in the chapter), a memory store is required so that this information can be recalled (retrieved) when required and applied when necessary. Psychologists often refer to the **'Model of Memory'** proposed by Atkinson and Shiffrin (1968), which suggested that information is managed first by a *short-term store*, but then in conjunction with a *long-term store*.

Short-term store

The short–term cognitive store has a limited capacity:

- It can store about seven items (or 'chunks') of information at a time, known as '7 *plus or minus 2*' (Miller 1956).
- It stores information for a few seconds only.

CASE EXAMPLE 3.2

Here is a string of digits to try and remember:

3   4   8   5   6   9   0   8   1   3   3   4   5   1   0   9   7   2   1   4

Cover them up and try recall as many as possible *in the right order.*

Now try again with a string of words:

banana   happiness   garage   popcorn   umbrella   noisy   catapult   hat

How many did you remember?

Is your short-term memory better with digits, or words that you can assign meaning to?

Once information has reached the short-term store, a process of encoding occurs and information can only be retained beyond a few seconds by 'rehearsal' (repeating over and over). Think in terms of a young child trying to quickly learn ten new spellings or their times tables just before a class test, or an adult saying a car number plate over and over to themselves after observing a hit and run car accident because they do not have a pen or other device to store it. Although it is unlikely to be more than seven 'items' that can be managed in the short-term store, some people are able to persevere with the task and keep the information in their short-term store better than others. However, everyone eventually loses the information in this store, unless it is transferred for storage in the *long-term store*.

Long-term store

In contrast to the short-term store, the long-term store keeps information for a much longer period of time. Information can be retained for hours, week, months or even years! In some cases, information is 'set' for life, to be recalled when necessary. As with the short-term store, some people are better able to do this than others. This store is different to the short-term store because it uses 'semantic coding', which attaches meaning to information. This is why the context of critical events (for example, the information surrounding hearing bad news or witnessing a shocking scene) or memories that evoke specific emotions (for example, being given a meaningful gift or hearing exciting news) are much more easily retained. We often remember many details in such circumstances in a precise way, which is called 'flashbulb memory' and it is a useful phenomenon (especially when asked to give an account as a witness).

The problem with Atkinson and Shiffrin's model of the short-/long-term store is that it provides an overly simplistic outline of how our memory is implicated in the processing of information. This was highlighted by Baddeley (1986, 1996), who suggested that there are broader cognitive structures and components that feed into our awareness of information, and how we remember it (and including the potential to *not* remember some information, i.e. forget). Baddeley described the system of managing information as our *'working memory'*.

Working memory

Baddeley and Hitch (1974) identified three interacting componants within the Working Memory Model (also note that Repovs and Baddeley (2006) added a fourth component, an **episodic buffer** to the model as an extra component):

- a **phonological loop** (for storing *speech-based information*)
- a **visual–spatial sketchpad** (for storing *visual information*)
- an **executive system** (for combining information from various sources to *solve problems and create plans*).

Through the Working Memory Model, we begin to integrate the idea of 'processing information' with *'consciousness'* (being able to generate mental images, concepts, ideas and mental manipulations) and *'attention'* (being able to increase attention to particular information over other information). It shows that there is a tendency to prioritise some information at times when we have a high volume of information to process; for example during exam time! This finite nature of the system explains why some information is *not retained* or forgotten to make way for more pertinent information (pertinent being more important to that particular learner at that time). The Working Memory Model idea helps us to understand how, during classroom learning, information is not simply absorbed. It also highlights the problems with teaching using rote methods, which are only effective if the learner is able to move new information to a long-term store efficiently and it remains a high priority to the learner to retain it. Gathercole and Pickering (2000) have linked individual differences in cognitive performance and attainment to the components of working memory.

A very small number of learners are fortunate to have a particular ability associated with memory called 'eidetic memory' (sometimes called 'photographic memory'). This type of memory allows a full, precise recollection of information but it is unusual, and learners who do not have this ability cannot use it to learn in this way.

Interference

Because the long-term store relies on attaching meaning to the information, there is potential for *distortion*. Distortion occurs because the links we made to the information we have processed are held more strongly than the information itself, which means that some of what we recall is reconstructed content to fit our own understanding.

When learners start to recall information, they first access *the meaning,* and there is potential for crossover into the **reconstructed content** rather than the *initially received* information. For example, if a pupil is asked to remember some key historical facts and then asked to recall them to write an essay, it is likely that there will be distortion based on how that individual interpreted those events, and this can lead to a permanently altered recall unless they are corrected.

The potential for crossover can have an enormous influence on learning, and teachers must take care with: a) *how information is presented,* and b) the *context that the information is presented in* at the time when it is initially coded. There is potential for eventual information-retrieval inaccuracy or failure. Crossover is more likely to occur when information is given at an *excessive rate or pace*, and so teachers should also consider the need to make learners aware that 'cramming' or 'booster' activities may do more harm than good. Dorfberger *et al.* (2007) have suggested that younger children experience interference less than older children and adults. This may well relate to their lack of experience and prior assumptions. This helps explain why young children are more able to learn through rote methods.

Inference

Inference relates to *inter*ference, but is associated more with how we learn when information is restricted or limited. As considered earlier in the chapter, some learners naturally have better memory skills, but this facility allows the learner to make use of prior knowledge which helps us to 'fill in the gaps' in our understanding. Some people end up relying on inference more than others to make sense of new knowledge and experiences.

The contribution of Piagetian theory

The most well-known contribution to our understanding of cognition came from Jean Piaget. Piaget suggested that information can be 'clustered' to organise and then use information (Piaget and Inhelder 2000). Human beings prefer to find short cuts (a heuristic approach) to take on new knowledge quickly so as to cope in a world where we are bombarded continually with direct and sensory experience. As discussed earlier in the chapter, we rarely escape the bombardment. Piaget proposed that there are mental structures that are the *building blocks of thought* and *learning* new things, which psychologists call 'schemas'. In early childhood 'schemas' are open and flexible, in light of the fact that most experiences and information are novel at a young age. Here a high level of *inference* is required until a basic, stable platform of concrete understanding develops. Children can have quite large gaps in their knowledge but still manage to understand an awful lot. However, as the child develops, the 'schemas' become more and more complex, and by adulthood most learners are able to engage in sophisticated, high-level thinking because their mental structures are bolstered by a good bedrock from earlier schema formation. Piaget also suggested that, because a learner develops a complex matrix of mental structures as they progress through childhood, by *adulthood,* abstract thought, hypothesis testing and self-awareness as a learner is possible (able to think through the impact of information, ideas and learning by themselves). Of course, Piaget's ideas depend on agreement that children's cognition develops through a **sequence of developmental stages**. More recently, there has been evidence collated to demonstrate that children can carry out sophisticated and mature thinking and reasoning at much earlier ages than Piaget conceived (Siegler and Alibali 2005). *If you would like to learn more about Piaget's ideas (and in particular his 'Stage Theory'), see Chapter 7 for details and also the links and related literature signposted in the 'Extended Research Tasks' section at the end of this chapter.*

Metacognition

Metacognition is a concept that is becoming better known in education settings. Pupils with good metacognition tend to be better learners and do well in their education (Flavell 1979). Psychologists use the term 'metacognition' to mean the **awareness a learner has of their own cognitive processes**: i.e. awareness of their thinking, their strategies and approaches to learning. It is also a term applied to how the learner *identifies* and *overcomes barriers and blocks to their learning*.

There are three basic forms of metacognition:

- **metamemory** – the learner can recognise the best strategy for remembering for a given task most effectively

- **metacomprehension** – the extent to which the learner recognises how well they are understanding the information being presented and why they may fail to understand

- **self-regulation** – the learner can make adjustments to ensure that they take up more successful strategies on their own (when less effective learning is taking place).

Metacognition is not necessarily a *conscious* act, only a *potentially* conscious and controllable activity (Pressley *et al.* 1987).

The characteristic of a 'good learner' is that the learner is able to direct their own learning through the three forms of metacognition outlined previously, in response to the *self-monitoring* they engage with when learning. Good learners have developed an awareness that comes from being in touch with their learning abilities and weaknesses, but they also make efforts to *affect change* in their way of managing information and their thinking in response to their successes and failures. Self-monitoring, awareness and response have links to **learner motivation**, which will be discussed more in Chapter 5.

Teachers can support learners to improve how they learn by employing techniques such as **'overlearning'** (deliberately reviewing information but with a focus on metacognitive thinking). Children can be helped to develop their metacognition by teachers teaching them to engage in *'self-talk'* (for example, children being taught to regularly ask themselves; what am I learning and why? What are the strategies I am using and how effective are they? What can I do to improve my learning?), and *talking to others* about their thought processes.

REFLECTION BOX 3.4   Reflection point

■   How often do you engage in 'self talk'?

■   Do you find talking out loud to *others* easier and more helpful than thinking through your learning using 'self-talk'?

■   Do you find that articulating your ideas to yourself or out loud is enough to move your learning forward, or is a 'knowledgeable expert teacher' more important to you?

Not all children will respond well to attempts to encourage independent metacognitive thinking. Some children are naturally more passive and will want to develop their thinking and understanding as an 'apprentice', or within a socio-cultural frame (watching and learning from others rather than grappling with information and knowledge by themselves). Teachers need to be flexible about how they manage learners, taking account where possible of how individuals prefer to process information.

In summary, the information-processing approach has provided a theoretical and practical way of exploring the ways in which children's thinking changes (i.e. the study of specific *processes* and *representations*) but it does not take into account other important factors relating to thinking and learning, such as **motivation** (reason to engage in behaviour) and **affect** (feeling or emotion), which are discussed more in Chapter 5 ('Motivation – is it the key to learning?') and Chapter 4 ('The complex interplay between cognition and emotion').

In this chapter we have focussed on the information-processing approach which is the most widely applied idea about cognition. However, there are *other ideas about cognition* that do not share the assumption that thinking and learning arises from symbolic representations and discrete processes. These are: ***ecological theories*** (which consider cognition as resulting from the environmental factors and their structure), ***neuroscientific ideas*** (which provide explanations of cognition in terms of neural functioning), ***social constructivist theory*** (how children's experiences underlie their cognition) and ***sociocultural theory*** (that communication, thinking and learning are shaped by a culture that are jointly negotiated and constructed). These approaches are considered at different points in this book.

EXTENDED RESEARCH TASKS

This book will help you to develop a broader understanding of the information-processing approach:

■ Haefner, K. (2011). *Evolution of Information Processing Systems: An Interdisciplinary Approach for a New Understanding of Nature and Society* (2nd Edition). Berlin: Springer Publishing Company.

A good basic introduction to the 'the nature of reality' is provided in:

■ Foster, J. (2013). *Surfing Realities: A Practical Guide to Understanding the Nature of Reality and How to Enhance Yours.* Bloomington: Balboa Press.

Turing's ideas about the possibilities of computers attaining a state of cognition are explained more in this book:

■ Petzold, C. (2008). *The Annotated Turing: A Guided Tour through Alan Turing's Historic Paper on Computability and the Turing Machine.* Chichester: Wiley.

You can find more information about eidetic memory in this article:

■ Martin, C. (2003). Memorable Outlier. *Current Biology*, **23** (17), pp. 731–733. DOI: 10.1016/j. cub.2013.08.027.

To learn more about value of Piaget's theory:

■ Inhelder, B., De Caprona, D. and Cornu-Wells, A. (Eds) (2014). *Piaget Today* (Psychology Revivals. 2nd Edition). Hove: Psychology Press.

References

Atkinson, R. C. and Shiffrin, R. M. (1968). Human Memory: A Proposed System and its Control Processes. In K. W. Spence and J. T. Spence (Eds), *The Psychology of Learning and Motivation*. New York: Academic Press.

Baddeley, A. D. (1986). *Working Memory*. Oxford: Clarendon Press.

Baddeley, A. D. (1996). Exploring the Central Executive. *Quarterly Journal of Experimental Psychology*, **49**, pp. 5–28.

Baddeley, A. D. and Hitch, G. J. (1974). Working Memory. In G.H. Bower (Ed.), *The Psychology of Learning and Motivation: Advances in Research and Theory. Vol. VIII.* New York: Academic Press.

Black, P. and Wiliam, D. (1990). *Inside The Black Box: Raising Standards through Classroom Assessment.* London: GL Assessments Limited.

Dorfberger, S., Adi-Japha, E. and Karni, A. (2007). *Reduced Susceptibility to Interverence in the Consolidation of Motor Memory before Adolescence.* Open-access article (PloS One, 2, e240) Available online at www.plosone.org/article/info%3Adoi%2F10.1371%2Fjournal.pone.0000240 (accessed 4 February 2014).

Flavell, J. H. (1979). Metacognition and Cognitive Monitoring: A New Area of Cognitive-Developmental Inquiry. *American Psychologist,* **34**, pp. 906–911.

Gathercole, S. E. and Pickering, S. J. (2000). Working Memory Deficits in Children with Low Achievements in the National Curriculum at Seven Years of Age. *British Journal of Educational Psychology,* **70**, pp. 177–194.

Gathercole, E., Packiam Alloway, T., Willis, C. and Adams, A. M. (2006). Working Memory in Children with Reading Disabilities. *Journal of Experimental Child Psychology,* **93**, pp. 265–281.

Geary, D. C. (2005). Role of Cognitive Theory in the Study of Learning Disability in Mathematics. *Journal of Learning Disabilities,* **38**, pp. 305–307.

Leather, C. V. and Henry, L. A. (1994). Working Memory Span and Phonological Awareness Tasks as Predictors of Early Reading Ability. *Journal of Experimental Child Psychology,* **58**, pp. 88–111.

McLean, J. F. and Hitch, G. H. (1999). Working Memory Impairments in Children with Specific Mathematics Learning Difficulties. *Journal of Experimental Child Psychology,* **74**, pp. 240–260.

Miller, G. A. (1956). The Magical Number 7 Plus or Minus 2: Some Limits on Our Capacity for Processing Information. *Psychology Review,* **63**, pp. 81–97.

Newell, A. and Simon, H. A. (1972). *Human Problem Solving.* Englewood Cliffs, NJ: Prentice Hall.

Passolunghi, M. C., Vercelloni, B. and Schadee, H. (2007). The Precursors of Mathematics Learning: Working Memory, Phonological Ability and Numerical Competence. *Cognitive Development,* **22**, pp. 165–184.

Piaget, J. and Inhelder, B. (2000). *The Psychology of the Child* (2nd Edition). New York: Basic Books.

Pressley, M., Borkowski, J. G. and Schneider, W. (1987). Cognitive Strategies: Good Strategy Users Coordinate Metacognition and Knowledge. In R. Vasta and G. Whitehurst (Eds), *Annals of Child Development,* **4**. Greenwich, CT: JAI Press.

Repovs, G. and Baddeley, A. D. (2006). Multi-Component Model of Working Memory: Explorations in Experimental Cognitive Psychology. *Neuroscience Special Issue,* **139**, pp. 5–2 1.

Searle, J. R. (2004). *Mind: A Brief Introduction.* Oxford: Oxford University Press.

Siegler, R. S. and Alibali, M. W. (2005). *Children's Thinking* (4th Edition). Upper Saddle River, NJ: Prentice Hall.

Swanson, H. L. and Beebe-Frankenberger, M. (2004). The Relationship between Working Memory and Mathematical Problem Solving in Children at Risk and not a Risk for Serious Math Difficulties. *Journal of Educational Psychology,* **96**, pp. 471–491.

Turing, A. M. (1950). Computing Machinery and Intelligence. *Mind,* **49***,* pp. 433–460.

Vernon, P. E. (1987). *Speed of Information Processing and Intelligence.* Norwood, NJ: Ablex.

4

The complex interplay between cognition and emotion

The psychological ideas in this chapter
■ the 'universality' of emotion
■ mentalising
■ the physiology of emotion
■ emotional intelligence
■ affect
■ empathy
■ sociopathy.

This chapter will take forward the ideas presented in the previous chapter about **cognition and metacognition** to consider how thinking and reasoning is influenced by **emotion**. The study of emotion is an important topic in psychology, but within education studies it is less prominent. Here, it is argued that an appreciation of the topic of emotion is crucial to your study of education if you are to develop a fuller understanding of the process of learning, and, within this chapter, it will be explained why. At the start of the chapter some basic ideas about 'emotion' will be presented, followed by a discussion of why it is important for those involved in the study of education to take account of 'emotional states'. There will also be a consideration of the ways that emotion impacts on thinking and rational thought as part of an explanation of the process of learning. Finally, there will be a consideration of how we can apply our understanding of emotion in the context of effective teaching and learning.

Some basic ideas about emotion

The emotional state of the learner tends to be underappreciated by educational professionals, yet, in contrast; psychologists are extremely interested in emotion because of its position as *a predominant characteristic of human behaviour*. Our present emotional state can influence our ability to concentrate on a task or how we view the situation we are in. For example, learning can be obstructed by negative emotion on the part of the learner and this also makes the job of teaching far more difficult for the professional (think in terms of the pupil who has suffered a bereavement or loss and is unable to focus and concentrate on the task at hand, or the angry and frustrated pupil who is unwilling to take part in the lesson and engage with what is being taught). Emotion is also strongly connected with **motivation** (see Chapter 5) and so by knowing more about how learners experience emotion, and express it, professionals working with pupils will be better equipped to manage learning and organise appropriate learning environments.

Within this book we consider some core psychological ideas, and emotion is one theme that it is important to include. However, in order to explain the impact of emotion on learning, there first needs to be some attention to some basic theories and ideas around 'human emotionality' and 'the physiology of emotion' – **what emotion is and how it is expressed**.

Human emotionality

Human emotionality theory proposes that all humans have the capacity to feel and display emotion. Humans are said to have at least six basic emotions (happiness, surprise, fear, sadness, anger, disgust and contempt) and humans can have each of these internal states regardless of age, gender, culture or social class. The theory of the '*universality of emotion*' was first proposed by Charles Darwin (Darwin 1872) and was more fully researched by anthropologist Paul Ekman. Ekman visited different countries across the world (including remote tribes of people) and disseminated his findings about emotions to the psychology field. (*To find out more about Ekman's work, see the related literature signposted in the 'Extended Research Tasks' section at the end of this chapter.*) Although there have since been disagreements about the exact *number* of standard emotions that humans can experience, the idea of universality (that we have the ability to experience the same basic set of emotions) proposed by Ekman (Ekman and Friesen 1971) is generally accepted.

REFLECTION BOX 4.1   Understanding yourself first

Think for a moment about Paul Ekman's six basic emotions – **happiness**, **surprise**, **fear**, **sadness**, **anger**, **disgust and contempt**.

- Have you felt all these emotions yourself?

- Can you think of an example of when you have felt each of these emotions linked to being a learner (as a pupil in school or as a student at university)?

Ekman's work also suggested that the human ability to recognise and interpret emotions in others is innate (something we are born to do). Research by Simon Baron-Cohen and co-researchers suggests that humans are skilled in recognising the mental and emotional states in others ('mentalising') and they do so by reading facial expression (Baron–Cohen *et al.* 1996) and gaze (Baron–Cohen and Cross 1992). Perhaps, then, it should be easy for teachers to be able to recognise basic emotions in pupils, for example if their pupil is happy, and be empathic when they sense that their pupil is sad or fearful.

REFLECTION BOX 4.2   Reflection point

- How easy do you find it to recognise basic emotions in others?

- Can you identify when a friend or family member is happy? Is it clear when they are angry? Is it easy to know when they are disgusted?

There is the opposing view that mental states are wholly private, and that humans can only *infer* an understanding of another person's emotions from observing general behaviour (Premack and Woodruf 1978), that it is possible for the learner to mask their true feelings from their teacher if they so desire.

Whichever view you take about the ability of humans to recognise emotion, it is clear that we must make assumptions about a learner's emotional state because we can never truly know for sure *exactly* how they are feeling. For example, early years teachers learn quickly that a crying child does not always mean a 'sad' child – e.g. if there are no tears it may likely be an expression of anger, or a manipulation strategy that even very young children are capable of. Care must be taken so that the teacher does not automatically modify their own behaviour and teaching strategies to take account of a perceived emotional state of the learner, or change an effective teaching approach because of a well-meaning attempt to accommodate a learner's emotional state. In fact, any attempt to demystify the emotions of a learner has the potential to distract the educator away from their planned teaching objectives. Therefore, the teacher must always find a balance between being led by the emotional needs of the learner and the potential for misreading these emotions.

For many educators, emotion falls within a pastoral rather than educational remit, seen as something that they have to do alongside their teaching role. Teachers often avoid exploring emotion too much in the school day and rarely go beyond being a 'listener' or offering discrete advice when the emotional state is so significantly elevated that it is obviously impacting on learning. But, when supporting learning or managing learner environments, teachers also should appreciate that there are much more subtle and consistent ways that the emotional state of a learner can influence their pupil's ability to think and rationally consider new information. This could include 'emotional hijacking', which will be discussed later in the chapter.

Although it may seem that the learner's true emotional state is difficult to gauge, there are ways that information can be gained through applying the idea of **micro-expressions**. Micro-expressions occur when a person is trying to conceal their true emotional reaction. Momentary, involuntary facial expressions are always presented instantaneously and last for only a fraction of a second (yet are still observable!) before the presentation of the *false expression* they want others to see. This is more common in *'high-stakes' situations* (when the person feels that their true feelings would create internal anxiety or an external negative response). An example of a 'high-stakes' situation would be where a pupil is given a detention – they may not wish for the teacher to gain insight into how it has really made them feel, or may wish to maintain a bravado with their peers. The primary emotion they would feel (disappointment or anger) is displayed momentarily before the emotional expression they *want to display* (ambivalence) appears. Once you are aware of this phenomenon then it is easy to recognise a micro-expression when it happens and it gives you a huge insight into the true feelings of others. It is an incredible powerful tool for teachers to possess.

The physiology of emotion

In order to understand more about the impact of emotion on thinking and reasoning, we need to consider first what we know about the physiology of emotion – what it is and where it 'comes from'. Several brain structures play a role in how emotion is felt and expressed by the

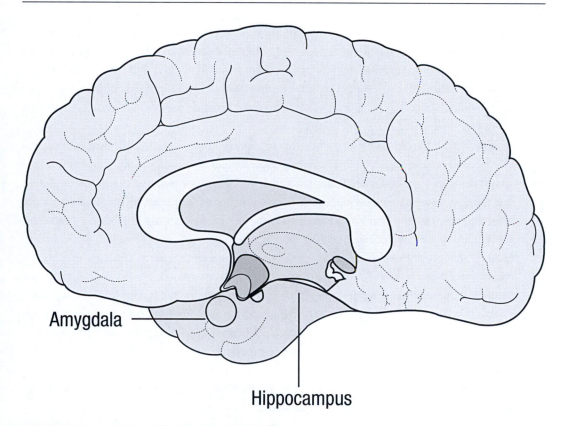

FIGURE 4.1 The amygdala and hippocampus areas of the brain
Taken from www.demneuropsy.com.br (accessed 26 March 2014).

individual. This chapter does not intend to provide a comprehensive overview of the brain (that is the job of neuropsychology textbooks!), but it will instead explain the basic areas that are implicated in feeling and responding to emotion.

Within the central area of the brain are certain structures that we know, from neuropsychological research, are important for emotion. In the central area of the brain is the **limbic system**, which is thought to have the primary responsibly for emotion. The **amygdala** is the particular area that is tasked with managing external stimuli relating to emotion, and it is connected to another brain area called the **hippocampus** (an area that manages memory) so that emotional expression and response is remembered, and recalled when required.

Brain studies look at inherited differences in brains and after brain injury, making comparisons to 'normal' brains (see Chapter 2 for a fuller account of how brain studies have informed our understanding). It is through brain studies that we have learned how important the limbic system and amygdala are for managing emotion. One famous study described how a building worker called Phineas Gage received a traumatic brain injury when an iron bar entered his brain (Damasio 1994). Much of Phineas's cognitive function continued to operate as before, but he was unable to regulate his emotion, becoming wilful and difficult around others. It is through making the link between the permanent changes to the damaged brain areas and relating this to changes in emotionality (with this case and others) that has helped neuropsychologists map which particular areas of the brain are responsible for different aspects of emotional function.

There is a hormone that is important for the regulation of emotion – **cortisol**, whose production and regulation can be linked to learner behaviour. Cortisol is secreted by the **adrenal gland**. Our levels of cortisol naturally fluctuate (increasing and reducing throughout the day), but more so as we encounter stressful or relaxing situations. In particular, an elevated cortisol level leads to us feeling anxious and compels us to respond with some sort of action. For example, when a threatening situation unfolds there is an increase in cortisol secretion, which in turn leads to changes to blood pressure and insulin levels, triggering anxiety. If we are mildly anxious we will begin to modify our behaviour (or make changes to our environment) in response to the increasing cortisol in our system in an attempt to stabilise the level. However, when we enter a moderate to highly anxious state then a much higher level of cortisol is secreted, instigating what is called the 'fight/flight response'. When we reach this point, we have entered a heightened state of anxiety where there are two predominant reactions – 'fight' (behaviour that manifests as 'a challenge' to what is creating the fear) and 'flight' (behaviour that manifests as procrastination or avoidance). Knowledge of this physiological process is important for a better understanding of human behaviour. It allows educators to recognise that an altered physiological state in pupils may lead to behaviour changes or more negative attitude.

Within the classroom there is frequent potential for 'learner anxiety' (through being faced with a worrying or unpleasant task or situations). It may help teachers if they recognise that behaviour and actions can be linked to an unconscious wish to stabilise cortisol secretion, and an awareness of the potential for the 'fight/flight response' may help teachers see that behaviour can have an internal causation which is individual to that pupil and not necessarily linked to their teaching methods.

What happens in the child's early emotional life can also have an impact on their later behaviour in the classroom. Studies have shown that babies who are exposed to stressful situations for too long or too often in their early years may have their brain 'flooded' with too much cortisol, which can lead to impaired cortisol regulation. Children who fall into this category can become indifferent to external stressors (unresponsive to external stimulus) or display a disproportionate response to stressful situations (with seemingly chaotic responses to external stimulus). Sudheimer (2009) has reported that in older children and adults (as occurs in Cushing's disease) when regulation fails and cortisol is hyper secreted, significant emotional changes occur, including depression. These are extreme situations, but teachers should be aware of how significant the influence of cortisol can be.

REFLECTION BOX 4.3   Reflection point

- Can you think of a time when you were feeling particularly emotional, whilst in a learning situation or about your academic workload?

- Was there an impact on your ability to learn (and, in particular, your attention to tasks)?

- Did you 'attack' the situation (worked harder to complete the task) or 'avoid' the situation (become distracted or do something else)?

The ways that emotion impacts on thinking and rational thought

The previous section in this chapter considered the role of cortisol and how it can impact on learner behaviour. At this point we need to consider the ideas of Daniel Goleman. Goleman has made an important contribution in psychology with his comprehensive 'theory of emotion', in which he described emotion as intimately connected with cognitive matters (Goleman 1995). He proposed that the amygdala (a key brain area for emotion, as described earlier in the chapter) had a tendency, in times of stress, to override other brain areas associated with rational thought, which he called 'emotional hijacking' (ibid). Goleman also provided a theoretical model of 'two minds' (the rational and emotional), which helps explain that, although cognition and emotion are seen as distinct, conceptually separable processes, they can influence one another. He also proposed that there is an emotional dimension to intelligence that can be measured, and he called this **emotional intelligence** (an 'Emotional Quotient'). *If you would like to take a test to find out your Emotional Quotient score, see the links and related literature signposted in the 'Extended Research Tasks' section at the end of this chapter.*

Goleman's ideas have been criticised for lacking empirical support (Fernández-Berrocal and Extremera 2005) and for promoting a stereotypical view that should not be consistently applied to all people (Elder 1997). However, Goleman's view of the importance of emotion on learning and behaviour is a helpful starting point for educators to think more about the idea that cognition and emotion do not function in isolation. Emotion does influence the learner's cognitive process, especially when their emotions are felt strongly and, by being aware of this, teachers can help child to understand this connection too.

Affect

Daniel Goleman was not the first theorist to propose that emotion and cognition are inter-linked. Early philosophers used the term 'affect' instead of emotion. It was recognised that there is a *physiological predisposition* to behaviour. Baruch Spinoza (later Benedict de Spinoza, 1632–1677) was a Dutch philosopher who was one of the first to speak of 'affect' (or 'affectio'), of which there were three aspects;

- desire (*cupiditas*) or appetite (*appetitus*)
- pleasure (*laetitia*)
- pain or sorrow (*tristetitia*).

Spinoza provided a comprehensive list of emotions (such as love, hatred, hope, fear, envy and compassion). In identifying different emotions, Spinoza asserted that emotion is a key feature of being human and is an internal response (feelings of pleasure, pain or sorrow) which arises in response to external stimuli (desire or appetite).

There have been two views of 'affect': the **traditional, 'post cognitive' theory of affect** and the **'separate systems' view of affect** (suggested by Zajonc 1980). The original, 'traditional' view is that emotion occurs as a result of cognition, and that emotion is always a response rather than something that stimulates thinking or behaviour. The more recent *'separate systems'* view is that affect and cognition are controlled by two *separate* systems in the brain. With this view, affect is not always post-cognitive (where affect and cognition come into conflict, the *affective* reaction is *primary* and *stronger*). In a practical sense, this means that learners have an automatic tendency to allow affect to dominate over rational thought, as with Goleman's 'emotional hijacking'. Whether a teacher takes a traditional or 'separate systems' view, they should take into account the *potential* for an affective reaction to dominate in the classroom, which would help them to pre-empt the possibility of an obstructed process of learning if learner emotions are running high.

Inference in emotion and learning

Emotion also plays a support role to cognition. Forgas (1995) considered affect to be a *heuristic* cue (meaning that 'feelings' and 'intuition' play a part in learning), filling in the gaps in understanding when logic alone is not enough to make sense of things. There are times when we cannot use rational thought to understand everything, particularly with regard to social situations. As discussed in the previous chapter, young children tend to be skilled at learning language and constructing knowledge in a very short space of time with limited experience, by using a process of *'inference'* (like being able to know what a finished jigsaw puzzle looks to be with a number of pieces still missing). Although inference is utilised, perhaps teachers should value it more and encourage pupils to retain, develop and use their feelings and intuition more as an effective support strategy for learning and also as a broader life skill.

Applying our understanding of emotion in the context of effective teaching and learning

So far in this chapter we have looked at some core ideas about emotion and how it impacts on thinking and rational thought. Now, we will consider how we can apply this understanding to education contexts. Earlier in this chapter we considered the idea that most pupils should (to some degree) recognise the emotions of their peers or their teacher (known as 'mentalising'). But why is the ability to read emotional states so important in learning situations? As you will appreciate, most learning happens, not as a 1:1 activity, but in a classroom (a social, populated space). Being able to recognise how others are feeling is an important skill required for effective relationships and social interactions when pupils are being educated in a class in the school community. If a pupil (or even a teacher) cannot pick up on cues that allow interpretations of the mental state of others, then learning becomes difficult. Some children are highly skilled at reading emotional cues, but other children are less skilled. Most children are born able to recognise emotions in others, but some children need to be taught how to do this. Some children will always find it difficult to read emotional cues and recognise emotions despite being given instructions in how to do it (this is a characteristic of children who are autistic).

Empathy

Not being able to recognise emotions in others is less problematic than the ability to *respond to the emotions of others*. Baron-Cohen and Wheelwright's (2004) self-report questionnaire is one tool which can be used to measure an ability to empathise. *If you would like to take a test to find out your Empathising Quotient score, see the links and related literature signposted in the 'Extended Research Tasks' section at the end of this chapter.* Genuine **empathic response** can be difficult to teach as it relies on being able to a) recognise what another person is feeling, b) genuinely care how that person feels, and c) a desire to modify one's own behaviour to take account of the emotional state of other people.

Within the population there are people who can read the emotions of others but are unable (or choose not to) modify their own behaviour based on what they have inferred about the emotional state of others. These people are known to psychologists as 'sociopaths'. Stout (2006) has presented an estimate that sociopathy is present in roughly 4 per cent of the population. Clearly, this group will not automatically have a reduced ability to learn but they may be more difficult to manage when being taught in social situations.

Mood

Although there is the idea that emotional state is linked to a person's temperament (Chess and Thomas 1996), emotion can fluctuate depending on what the person is thinking and their perception of what is happening to them at that time. This is known as **mood**. A pupil who is in a positive mood may well make different choices to another pupil who is in a 'bad mood'. Equally, a pupil can begin a day in one mood, but this can switch quickly depending on various factors (for example, recent interactions with others, physical health or mental state). It is important to consider mood in the context of learning because a positive mood allows for increased creativity and spontaneous ideas in learners (Isen *et al.* 1987; Davis 2009). Also, behavioural changes may occur when mood shifts (for example, a positive mood will allow a pupil to feel less anxious and so result in more stable cortisol production). Finally, a positive mood helps pupils (and teachers) rate others around them and situations more positively. Teachers should be aware that more attention is paid by pupils to information that relates closely to how they feel (**'mood congruence'**) and they are more likely to relate/displace a positive mood to their current learning task. Teachers can use this as a 'pairing up' strategy; for example, if pupils are in a good mood they are more likely to feel positive about a project being given to them.

Rigidity

This 'pairing', described above, occurs generally where prior experience has a connection to how it made us feel, which we transfer to our current state. If our prior experience was positive, this can be a helpful association, but if we have a negative attribution (because a previous situation was unpleasant) then this may cause a barrier to learning. Pupils may use 'stereotypes' of particular situations and then to the observer behave in a seemingly irrational way. This manifests as **rigidity of thinking**. For example, a pupil may have had an unpleasant situation arise previously with a male teacher, which could generalise to become a dislike of all male teachers. Teachers should encourage pupils to rationally consider new experiences or activities as independent to previous ones, to avoid old emotions influencing how they feel and approach tasks in the present.

REFLECTION BOX 4.4   Reflection point

Look back to the last 'Reflection Point'. You were asked to think of a time when you were feeling emotional in a learning situation, or about your academic workload.
   Now answer the following questions:

■   What helped you overcome the impact?

■   Did you manage to do this yourself, or did you need another person to support you?

When supporting pupils, teachers may use effective teaching strategies that support both cognition and emotion. For example, a teacher may use **positive reinforcement** (*if you would like to find out more about positive reinforcement, see Chapter 5 and the links and related literature signposted in the 'Extended Research Tasks' section at the end of this chapter*) and **praise** (Swinson and Harrop 2012) to create a positive emotional climate, which in turn reduces the potential for 'emotional hijacking' to occur. A **positive emotional climate** has been found to be a critical factor to both teachers' and students' emotional well-being and cognitive performance (Hamre and Pianta 2001). Less positive classrooms have been found to have *lower levels of achievement* and *greater conflict* (Hamre and Pianta 2005).

   This chapter has explained the ways that emotion and cognition interrelate, which must both be considered *together* rather than as independent aspects. Yet, within the current performative, neoliberal context of education (Lyotard 1984; Garrett and Forrester 2012), emotion sits in the shadow of cognition and tends to be seen as secondary (and perhaps, in hierarchical terms, to be less valuable) in the process of learning. This chapter has argued that emotionality (the emotions of pupils, their emotional state and emotional response, and the skills associated with reading emotion in others) are important features of being human and must not be overlooked by teachers as something that is pastoral or therapeutic (for a person other than the educator to consider). Emotion is an essential feature of learning and must be considered as such by educationalists.

EXTENDED RESEARCH TASKS

Paul Ekman's work on emotion is explained fully in:

- Ekman, P., Friesen, W. V. and Ellsworth, P. (1983). *Emotion in the Human Face: Guidelines for Research and an Integration of Findings*. Cambridge: Cambridge University Press.

You can find out your emotional intelligence score online, as there are a number of free tests available; however, they are not necessarily validated. Instead, visit The Emotional And Social Competency Inventory (ESCI) webpage:

- www.haygroup.com/leadershipandtalentondemand/ourproducts/item_details.aspx?itemid=58&type=1

To find out more about positive reinforcement and how it can be applied practically in schools read:

- Crone, D. A. and Horner, R. H. (2003). *Building Positive Behavior Support Systems in Schools: Functional Behavioral Assessment*. New York: The Guilford Press.

References

Baron-Cohen, S. and Cross, P. (1992). Reading the Eyes: Evidence for the Role of Perception in the Development of a Theory of Mind. *Mind and Language*, **6**, pp. 173–186.

Baron-Cohen, S. and Wheelwright, S. (2004). The Empathy Quotient: An Investigation of Adults with Asperger Syndrome or High Functioning Autism, and Normal Sex Differences. *Journal of Autism and Developmental Disorders,* **34** (2), pp. 163–175.

Baron-Cohen, S., Riviere, A., Cross, P., Fukushima, M., Bryant, C., Sotillo, M., Hadwin, J. and French, D. (1996). Reading the Mind in the Face: A Cross-Cultural and Developmental Study. *Visual Cognition*, **3**, pp. 39–59.

Chess, S. and Thomas, A. (1996). *Temperament Theory and Practice*. New York: Brunner/Mazel.

Damasio, A. R. (1994). *Descartes' Error: Emotion, Reason, and the Human Brain*. New York: Grosset/Putnam.

Darwin, C. (1872). *The Expression of the Emotions in Man and Animals*. London: John Murray.

Davis, M. A. (2009). Understanding the Relationship between Mood and Creativity: A Meta-Analysis. *Organisational Behaviour and Human Decision Processes*, **108**, pp. 25–38.

Ekman, P. and Friesen, W. V. (1971). Constants across Cultures in the Face and Emotion. *Journal of Personality and Social Psychology*, **17**, pp. 124–129.

Elder, L. (1997). Critical Thinking: The Key to Emotional Intelligence. *Journal of Developmental Psychology*, **21** (1), pp. 40–51.

Fernández-Berrocal, P. and Extremera, N. (2005). About Emotional Intelligence and Moral Decisions. *Behavioral and Brain Sciences*, **28**, pp. 548–549.

Forgas, J. P. (1995). Mood and Judgment: The Affect Infusion Model (AIM). *Psychological Bulletin*, **117**, pp. 39–66.

Garratt, D. D. and Forrester, G. (2012). *Education Policy Unravelled*. London: Continuum.

Goleman, D. (1995). *Emotional Intelligence: Why it can Matter More than IQ*. London: Bloomsbury Publishing.

Hamre, B. K. and Pianta, R. C. (2001). Early Teacher-Child Relationships and the Trajectory of Children's School Outcomes through Eighth Grade. *Child Development*, **72** (2), pp. 625–638.

Hamre, B. K. and Pianta, R. C. (2005). Can Instructional and Emotional Support in the First-Grade Classroom Make a Difference for Children at Risk of School Failure? *Child Development*, **76** (5), pp. 949–967.

Isen, A. M., Daubman, K. A. and Nowicki, G. P. (1987). Positive Affect Facilitates Creative Problem Solving. *Journal of Personality and Social Psychology*, **52**, pp. 1,122–1,131.

Lyotard, J. (1984). *The Postmodern Condition: A Report on Knowledge*. Minneapolis: University of Minnesota Press.

Premack, D. and Woodruff, G. (1978). Does the Chimpanzee Have a Theory of Mind? *Behaviour and Brain Science*, **1**, pp. 515–526.

Stout, M. (2006). *The Sociopath Next Door*. New York: Broadway Books/Random House.

Sudheimer, K. D. (2009). The Effects of Cortisol on Emotion. A dissertation submitted for the degree of Doctor of Philosophy. The University of Michigan.

Swinson, J. and Harrop, A. (2012). *Positive Psychology for Teachers*. London: Routledge.

Zajonc, R. B. (1980). Feeling and Thinking: Preferences Need No Inferences. *American Psychologist*, **35** (2), pp. 151–175.

5

Motivation – is it a key to learning?

The psychological ideas in this chapter

- humanistic perspective: hierarchy of needs

- behaviourist perspective: classical and operant conditioning

- intrinsic and extrinsic motivation

- consideration of different strategies.

What is motivation?

The answer to this question has puzzled human thinkers for hundreds of years. For example, why do some people wake up and leap out of bed, ready for a day at school, work or university? In comparison, others may keep hitting the snooze button and end up starting their day off, sluggish and reluctant to 'have a go' at new experiences. It could be that their bodies are tired and they need to rest, but what if they have had the same amount of good sleep and they are going to the same place, and studying the same subject? Why do some people seem to be *more motivated than others?*

What is it that 'makes' these individuals behave in the way that they do? Is it something that is internal, like a switch inside the body that needs to the flicked to initiate the behaviour?

Or, is it is the external environment that forces the individuals to behave in this manner? These questions are often asked by psychologists but also by those of us who want to work with children or young people in an educationally orientated manner. Imagine if we could all understand exactly what motivation is!

A clearer understanding of the mechanism of motivation would help educators to support children in developing *positive* motivation towards their learning. Unfortunately, motivation is a little more complicated than that and before we can reach that supportive point, we need to look at the various types of motivation and theories that have been put forward first.

Psychologists have defined motivation as:

■ an internal state that arouses, directs and maintains behaviour (Woolfolk *et al.* 2008);

■ all of the pushes and prods (biological, social and psychological) that defeat our laziness and move us, either eagerly or reluctantly to action (Miller 1962).

This means that motivation is a *driver* of our actions. It is the *'thing'* that enables us to actively feed our bodies when hungry, to water it with fluids when thirsty; finally, it enables us to sit and read books for hours on end or write long essays on topics that we are not really interested in. Our behaviour can change in relation to the current goal that we have set ourselves, or that have been set by others, such as teachers, so that we can achieve them. For an example of some of these characteristic changes in behaviour see Table 5.1. Therefore, Gross (2010) suggests that it should be thought of as an amalgamation of biological, emotional, social and cognitive forces. In very basic terms, it is the reason *why* people behave in certain ways in everyday situations.

REFLECTION BOX 5.1   Understanding yourself first

Take a look at the two motivated and unmotivated columns of characteristics in Table 5.1 below. In relation to yourself as a learner:

■ Have you demonstrated any of these characteristics in your own learning?

■ Can you recall a task which you felt unmotivated to complete?

Consider the possible reasons as to why you felt unmotivated towards that particular task.

■ Was it due to internal reasons (e.g. yourself) or external reasons (e.g. teacher or setting)?

TABLE 5.1 Characteristics of learners

Motivated learners	Unmotivated learners
■ tend to choose more challenging tasks	■ opt for the tasks deemed easiest
■ often don't need encouraging to start tasks	■ often need to be coerced to get started
■ work with a positive attitude	■ work with a negative attitude towards the task or their own abilities
■ demonstrate effort and concentrate towards the tasks	■ demonstrate a resistance to applying themselves to completing the task
■ overcome difficult tasks by employing a range of different strategies	■ often give up quickly, especially if they feel the task is too 'difficult'
■ become determined to complete the task set.	■ are willing to leave the tasks unfinished.

Developing motivation

Early childhood involves vast amounts of learning and in general, children are eager to learn and initially very motivated too! For example, children at the age of one would not understand the expectations their parents held, in relation to their learning, so most of their behaviour is due to **intrinsic motivation**. This is the term psychologists use when referring to motivation that derives from *within* an individual. For example, babies want to learn because they want to understand the world they are in. They are eager to touch, smell and taste items so that they can make sense of what they are and how they may be able to use them. However, when children reach school age and are constrained by learning the topics that form part of the curriculum, it appears that '*some*' children become **extrinsically motivated** to gain the correct answers, or the best grades.

'Extrinsically' is a term used by psychologists that means an individual's motivation is *externally* driven. For example, they are only writing the essay because they have been instructed to do so by the teacher and if they don't follow through with the request they won't receive any verbal feedback/praise. This change in motivating forces/drivers: from intrinsic (internal) to extrinsic (external) is something that anyone working within educational settings needs to be aware of. The reason for this is that most research has shown that intrinsically motivated pupils tend to gain more from a learning task than those who are extrinsically motivated to complete it (Brophy 1997; Tapola and Niemivirta 2008). This could depend on the way the child sets about attempting to 'learn', what they perceive to be 'learning' (which we will look at in more detail in Chapter 7) and what goals or values they hold in relation to the learning task.

It is important to consider why some children's motivational force changes *from* intrinsically driven to being more *extrinsically dependent* within a classroom setting. Some academics have argued that it occurs because the curriculum becomes too distinct and different for children and that this means that they struggle to see the relevance of the learning being asked of them (Brophy 1997; Penn 2008). I am sure you will be able to recall an incident yourself where you have sat staring at an essay question wondering why on earth you have been asked to learn about a certain topic (e.g. about the philosophical arguments within the black plague era) when it appears to bear no relevance to a career working with children and young people in the twenty-first century. In those kinds of situations, it is easy to understand why some people lose motivation to complete the tasks set, which means they need to rely on extrinsic motivators to help them get through the work load.

REFLECTION BOX 5.2   Reflection point

Having looked at the different motivational forces, take a minute to consider why you have decided to study education.

- What is your driving force?

- Is it an *intrinsic* desire to learn about the education system and how professionals go about teaching and learning?

- Or, is it due to an *extrinsic* force, Such as the need to gain a degree so that you can gain employment within an educational setting somewhere?

- What if your motivation is a mixture of both?

In theory then, as educators, we should be able to extrinsically motivate all individuals; although the stark reality is that this option is actually very difficult to carry out for a number of reasons. One of them is that motivation (whether intrinsic or extrinsic) is *malleable*. This means that there are a number of events, or items, that can change an individual's motivational focus: every day, every task and even every minute or second of the day! For example, you were asked to consider your own motivational driver for studying education. If you came to the conclusion that I hope most students would – that you are intrinsically and extrinsically motivated – then what does that mean for your ability to focus on completing each individual task set?

There are a number of psychological theories that attempt to explain what influences our motivational drivers but this chapter will concentrate on the two main contenders: the humanistic and behaviourist perspectives. First to be discussed is the humanistic approach, which is thought to have been originally founded by Carl Rogers in his 1960s work. However, the humanistic theory of motivation that we are going to look at comes from Abraham Maslow and was actually published in 1943, well before Rogers developed the humanistic perspective altogether.

Humanism

In relation to *drivers* of our behaviour, humanistic psychologists, like Abraham Maslow (1943) believed that we are driven by our unique, personal needs that we *desire to have fully met*. To help explain how and why our motivational focus can shift so easily, Maslow described a hierarchy of needs, which tends to be portrayed in the shape of a pyramid in most textbooks (although, Maslow never stated this was how he intended us to perceive his hierarchy!). Regardless of this, Maslow did explicitly describe his hierarchy as containing 'levels' which usually must be met before an individual will be able to focus on the next level up the hierarchy. The first level starts off with a need (driver) to have all of our *physiological needs* met. This includes oxygen to breathe, food and drink to sustain physical activity and the ability to regulate our bodies, for example by maintaining homeostasis (e.g. temperature and elimination needs). Child development specialists have argued that these are *instinctual* needs that every child is biologically programmed to satisfy from conception.

Maslow continued by stating that, if the first level of physiological needs are being met in some way, then an individual may start to look at meeting the needs of the next level up the hierarchy. This second level focusses on our *safety needs*. Maslow believed this meant being protected from any possible harm, both *physically* and *psychologically*. Therefore, having a safe place to rest and sleep, and also being able to access environments that won't put us in potentially dangerous situations (e.g. having access to clean facilities meaning the risk of becoming seriously ill is substantially reduced).

The third level is centred on our *love* and *belonging needs*. Maslow proposed that these social needs are vitally important to our overall happiness and need to be the first ones met after ensuring that our physical and safety needs were secure. For example, this level involves receiving and giving love and attention to another individual. It is a need to develop trusting relationships that enable an individual to feel they belong to and are actively a part of a group (e.g. family unit, friendship groups, social groups like Brownies or Scouts and/or work groups of colleagues).

The next level, *esteem needs*, focusses on achieving the respect of others and developing a positive self-esteem and self-concept (see Chapter 6 for more details). This means understanding what our competence level is and being comfortable with it, in relation to the competence levels of the individuals around us. In other words, it relates to our social status and subsequent learning desires and curiosity about the world. If all of our lower levels are being met, then it is at this level that students will be intrinsically motivated to learn and develop their knowledge and skills. Therefore, this is an important level for educators, as if a learner has any unmet needs on the lower levels these will start to act as a 'blockage' that restricts the pupil from focussing and being motivated towards meeting their own learning needs.

According to Maslow, if an individual has managed to make their way up the hierarchy of needs and met the first four levels, then the last level to meet is termed *self-actualisation*. This refers to the *ultimate goal of human existence*: to be self-fulfilled and content; to reach the highest level of perceived personal development. Maslow was quick to note that most individuals continually strive to reach this level throughout their lifetime; but that only a relative few would actually achieve it. Possible examples of self-actualised individuals have been put forward, including Mother Theresa, Mahatma Gandhi and Nelson Mandela.

Overall, in relation to the hierarchy of needs, Maslow believed that we are driven by two different drivers. The first drives us in an animalistic fashion: to secure our basic survival (levels one, two and three). The other is an intrinsically driven desire to self-actualise (starting from level four and ultimately reaching level five). This means that most students today who live in Westernised, well-resourced countries) should be intrinsically motivated to learn; however, any individual who steps foot inside a classroom would understand that this statement does not always become a working reality!

According to Maslow, the reason why some people struggle to be 'motivated', to drive their behaviour towards reaching a higher level, is because one of the lower levels is not being met or is only being partially met. For example, a student may be attending a lecture (listening to an educationalist delivering an engaging talk) but they are not able to take on board everything that is being said, because on this particular occasion, they are simply hungry. Let's say, for simplicity, they missed breakfast because they got up late; in this instance, it wouldn't have a detrimental impact on the individual's overall survival. However, if this particular student was struggling to eat two or three basic meals per day (for various possible reasons) this would start to have a detrimental impact on their ability to even function at all!

The last example is rather extreme, but it is one worth considering when contemplating motivating children and young people. The lives of children differ enormously and in any role within education we simply don't have much control over what happens outside of schools or settings. However, within the classroom, we need to be aware of possible 'blockages' that could be placing restrictions on an individual child's ability to motivate themselves towards their learning goals (reaching levels four and five). Take a look at Table 5.2, which provides a variety of different examples of possible blockages at each level.

Although this theory has provided us with a firm understanding of how intrinsic motivation is developed, what it doesn't explain is why some people can overcome the

TABLE 5.2 The five levels of Maslow's 'hierarchy of needs' and example blockages for each level

Hierarchy of needs (motivators)	Possible blockage in students' lives
Level five: self actualisation	*struggling with any level below this one*
Level four: esteem needs	self-loafing, self-harming, lack of confidence in self, lack of respect from peers or colleagues, lack of interest in subject being studied, already gained the knowledge being taught
Level three: love and belonging	insecurely attached to a care giver, affectionless parent – child relationships, poor sibling bonding, peer to peer bullying
Level two: safety needs	instability in accommodation, poor housing, extreme weather conditions (e.g. floods, hurricanes etc.), subjected to neglect or abuse
Level one: physiological needs	hunger (starvation), thirst (dehydration), too hot or too cold, constipation, tired (exhausted), no access or time to carry out physical exercise and even having no opportunities to perform sexual activities can impact an adult's ability to function in certain ways!

Adapted from Gross (2010)

drawbacks of partially met needs and still be motivated in achieving other goals. For example, a photographer could put themselves in extreme danger in a bid to catch a clear picture of the 'eye' of a storm. This goes against the direct needs of level two (safety).

Additionally, a child may read a book every week because they want to collect the 'book worm' stickers that the teacher is giving out, even though this means having to endure the constant name calling and physical bullying outside of class from other children (thereby, not meeting level three or occasionally level two needs). In both of these examples, the individuals appear to be overriding their survival needs in attempts to reach higher ordered needs of *esteem* (e.g. the photographer may wish to use the picture as a way of showcasing his talents to others, and the child may wish to receive the verbal praise that the teacher gives when she hands out the stickers). However, there is another psychological perspective that provides an alternative way of understanding motivational forces: the *behaviouristic* approach to motivation.

Behaviourism

According to the behaviourist school of thought in psychology, the two individuals in the previous example (photographer and reading child) have been trained to become extrinsically motivated. Behaviourist psychologists believe that children are born as blank slates (or in Latin: *tabula rasa*) and that they must therefore learn everything after they are born. This also means that they must *learn to become motivated too*. According to this approach, children learn to respond to stimulus by producing responses on a trial and error basis. They subsequently learn which ones gain them the response they need. Take, for example, a new-born baby who feels intense hunger. They do not understand how to ask for milk or food yet so they respond with the only communication tool that they know of at this stage: intense crying or screaming. The parent or carer responds by providing the breast or bottle and once the child has started to feed, the feeling of hunger dissipates. If this occurs again and again, the child learns that feeling hungry can be overcome by crying out, which results in receiving a substance (milk) that if swallowed, will eventually take that feeling away!

A number of famous experiments have been carried out that have investigated this process of producing specific behaviour. Pavlov (1927) initially termed this process 'classical conditioning', which describes the process of *learning through association*. However, Pavlov's work involved an experiment with dogs and researchers were, at first, sceptical of whether it was transferable to human behaviour. To build on this, two behaviourist psychologists, Watson and Raynor, carried out one very famous experiment in 1920. The experiment is widely known as the **'Little Albert' experiment** and it was designed to see if Pavlov's original ideas about classical conditioning could be used to teach a child to be afraid of something and then to reverse the process and unlearn the developed phobia. However, the findings of the experiment also help us to understand why human beings become motivated to perform certain actions.

Watson and Raynor's experiment involved showing 'Little Albert' (who, at the start of the study, was nine months old) a number of items to assess how he responded to each one (e.g. white rat, dog, monkey, rabbit, cotton wool, burning newspaper and face masks). Once Watson was assured that the items did not cause any negative reactions, he chose to let Albert play with the white rat. He would then creep up behind him and strike a long steel bar with a hammer (making a very loud sound right behind Albert); this naturally made Albert feel very frightened. Over the course of seven more episodes involving the same process of rat and steel bar, Albert become motivated to physically remove himself from the situation whenever he saw the white rat appear.

Watson and Raynor published their findings and proclaimed that they had evidence of human beings learning (being motivated) to behave in certain ways due to the process of *classical conditioning*. They explained that, in the *pre-conditioning stage*, Little Albert showed the expected (desired) response to the sound of the steel bar being hit, which was fear. Once they knew this would occur whenever Little Albert heard the noise, they moved onto the *conditioning stage* (see Figure 5.1 for the various stages of classical conditioning). This involved introducing the white rat at the same time as making the loud bang with the metal bar. After seven repeats of this, Little Albert had progressed into the *post-conditioned stage*, where he would show immediate fear as soon as he saw the white rat. The steel bar was no longer needed, as he had learnt to associate the sight of the rat with the overwhelming feeling of fear that he had previously experienced.

The actual case about Little Albert was very interesting; for example, he not only *learnt to become afraid of white rats* but he also learnt to become *afraid of anything white* (including Watson, who had white hair!). Sadly, the researchers did not get the chance to remove the phobia from Little Albert (assuming that they intended to!), as his mother withdraw him from the study earlier than anticipated. On that note, the experiment has since been condemned due to the unethical practices involved (see Chapter 8 for further discussion on ethical research practices).

After Watson and Rayner had shown that conditioning could be carried out on human beings, there was an increase of psychological interest in the areas of motivation and behaviour. For example, Skinner (1935) moved the discussion on one step further, when he showed through his rat experiment that animals/people learn through the *consequences of their actions*, not because of the associations that they make with a stimulus. For example, within his experiment, he had designed a box (now widely known as the '*Skinner box*') that was connected to a food dispenser unit and also an electrical current. He placed a single rat within the box and waited until the rat accidently stood on the lever. This would then dispense food to the rat and eventually the rat learnt that standing of the lever meant that more often than not it would receive some kind of food (Skinner was adamant that the food should not appear every time, as, if it did, it would no longer offer a reward. Instead, it would become habitual). He used an electrical current to see if the rat would also learn how to switch it off! In fact, the rat was quick to pick up that should it receive a low frequency shock, it should seek out the lever (which could be moved around the box) and press it to stop the current. Skinner's experiments demonstrated that the animals had learnt to associate items but more importantly they had learnt that the consequences of their actions were much more important.

Skinner argued that if your behaviour or actions provide something pleasant then an individual is highly likely to repeat that behaviour or action again; in other words, they become *motivated* to repeat it (e.g. the rat pressed the lever and was pleasantly rewarded with food). He called his version of conditioning '*operant conditioning*'. Therefore, his theory was focussed on the consequences of our actions as they reinforce (drive) whether we repeat an action again. He proposed two types of reinforcements:

- *positive* reinforcement
- *negative* reinforcement.

Both types of reinforcement strengthen a behavior, making it more likely to occur again).

Pre-conditioned stage	steel bar struck	= fear shown
Conditioning stage	white rat + steel bar struck	= fear shown
Post-conditioning stage	white rat	= fear shown

FIGURE 5.1 Showing the experiment's progression

Positive reinforcement	Negative reinforcement
Behaviour is strengthened by **using a pleasant** experience.	Behaviour is strengthened by **removing an unpleasant** experience.
The same end result = behaviour is strengthened	

FIGURE 5.2 Showing that both types of reinforcement have the same impact on behaviour

Positive reinforcement means that your actions are likely to occur again due to receiving a positive experience from them (e.g. gaining a sticker, being praised, being paid, receiving a gift etc.).

Negative reinforcement means that your actions are reinforced because they stopped a negative experience from continuing or happening (e.g. getting a good grade at school means you may avoid receiving a parent's disapproving chat! Or a teenager may have been grounded by their parents so they decide to clean their bedroom in an attempt to make things better. Rather than positively rewarding the person for cleaning their room (e.g. giving them money), the parents may decide to 'unground' the teenager, thereby negatively reinforcing the action of cleaning their bedroom by removing the unpleasant action of being grounded.

First, remember that motivation is the *driver* of our actions so **punishments** work in the same way as reinforcements but they actually **weaken** our behaviour instead of strengthening it. When a teacher chooses to make the class stay in at break time because they haven't completed all the work that was set, they have chosen to use a punishment with the aim of preventing that negative behaviour from occurring again. When you consider both classical and operant conditioning, the behaviouristic approach can help to explain why people become motivated to act in particular ways. Furthermore, it offers us an explanation as to why some people become more extrinsically motivated as they start to desire the positive or negative reinforcements that are offered by others around them. Or, because they want to avoid the punishments that might be the consequence of carrying out an action. Recall the example at the start of this chapter, about the different ways that people wake up eager to get to school/work or the ones who struggle to wake up and actively get themselves out of bed. The motivators for these two alternatives could be both positive or negative reinforcement! As an example, being at school provides positive experiences, or being there may be a negative experience so staying in bed would be a negative reinforcement in that situation!

Strategies to improving motivation

Working with children and young people means that we have to encourage them to try new experiences which might not seem like a 'good idea' to them. Or, we need to motivate them into conforming to the rules of the classroom or to the role of being a 'good' pupil. This can make the job of working with this particular group of individuals quite challenging at times!

REFLECTION BOX 5.3   Reflection point

Earlier, I asked you to recall a time when you felt unmotivated about completing a task.

- How did you move past that point?

- How did you motivate yourself to complete it?

Consider whether you were able to complete the task because you found your own motivation from within, or whether you became motivated due to an external source. If it was due to yourself, 'finding' your motivation again:

- Had there been a blockage somewhere that later resolved?

If it was external:

- Did you seek out opportunities to remind yourself of the positive reinforcement that would be achieved when you had completed the task?

If you want to take a behaviourist approach, then you need to be as clear as possible about the actions that you want the pupil to perform. But, also be clear about the reinforcement that is on offer too. For example, let's say that you want the children to sit down quietly on the carpet while you read them a story. Make it clear, from the start, exactly what you mean by 'sitting quietly' and what the consequences of this action will achieve (e.g. a sticker, a 'high five' or just that it will make you feel very proud of them). It is quite common in schools today to provide this kind of praise or attention, certificates or stickers to motivate children and young people to behave in expected ways. Just be careful that you choose the appropriate consequence: allowing a child to choose their own stickers will work wonders with younger students but this will not be seen as a great reward for an older teenager!

Furthermore, if you take this approach with children, you must remember to use it *sparingly*. Too many rewards or constant showering of praise will eventually mean the child will start to see the reward or praise in a less 'positive' and 'valued' manner (Kohn

2001). Similarly, if using this system of extrinsically motivating children, you must be prepared to follow through with what you have promised. For example, in the sitting down quietly example earlier, you must be able to and be prepared to be observant of their actions. You cannot ask them to sit still while you read the story and then forget to watch their actions whilst you're reading! Although this is easily done, it will end up undermining your whole operant conditioning approach. Never underestimate the power of extrinsic rewards, as they usually provide lots of motivation to children to do exactly what you have asked them to do. However, if you fail to hand out the rewards fairly or when promised, the disappointment can also condition them into ignoring your next request for rewarded behaviours!

Trying to increase a child's intrinsic motivation is very difficult, as the whole notion rests *within* them and their engagement with the environment. However, reverting back to Maslow's hierarchy of needs guides you in being more attentive to what is going on around individual students. Sitting down and having a chat about what is currently happening within their lives can provide you with some much needed understanding. Although this is easier to acheive with younger children, teenagers are still willing to chat to other people when they really need to. If they don't want to discuss their lives with you, then bring in assistance from other adults around school or other services if need be (e.g. learning mentors, pastoral officers, heads of year, family support workers, parents or even services like Child and Adolescent Mental Health Services [CAMHS]).

It's important to note, especially in psychology, that there will always be numerous perspectives provided on most topics and it is up to you to choose which one you feel is the best fit for the area of concern you are looking at. Having worked within education for a number of years, both authors of this book feel that taking an eclectic approach is usually more beneficial to children and young people. This simply means taking aspects from different perspectives and making a *toolkit* that can be used within classrooms or settings. For example, in relation to motivation, Maslow's hierarchy of needs model helps us to understand why and how people become intrinsically motivated and the behaviouristic approach explains how and why individuals can become extrinsically motivated! If you draw on both of these perspectives, you can use aspects of both ideas to help understand why children may be unmotivated and you can also use aspects of both models to help re-motivate them.

The growing disparity with how children and young people live and develop can have a large impact on their motivational styles. For instance, parents can nurture a child's intrinsic motivation but at the same time, well-meaning parents can also accidentally develop a child's preference for extrinsic rewards by offering pocket money for completing chores or providing day outs for good school reports. As a professional working within the education system, you need to be mindful of what happens outside of the classrooms and what you are offering within it as incentives. In relation to this, children develop individual identities, personalities and preferences and these influence their motivational drivers.

EXTENDED RESEARCH TASK

There are a number of books that will help to develop your psychological awareness of motivation:

- Gross, R. (2010). *Psychology: The Science of Mind and Behaviour.* London: Hodder Education. (This is a good starting point for any education based student who wants to delve into psychological ideas further but who also wants an easy to read approach.)

- Woolfolk, A., Hughes, M. and Walkup, V. (2008). *Psychology in Education.* Harlow: Pearson. (They have written six different chapters on motivational theories.)

- Schunk, H. H., Pintrich, P. R. and Meece, J. L. (2013). *Motivation in Education: Theory, Research and Applications (4th Edition).* New York: Pearson. (A thorough account of the theoretical ideas and current research on motivation.)

Humanistic perspective

To gain a deeper understanding of Maslow's hierarchy of needs theory, read through his original journal article:

- Maslow, A. H. (1943). *A Theory of Human Motivation. Psychological Review,* **50**, pp. 370–396.

Behaviourist perspective

As above, to gain a deeper understanding of the behaviourist perspective, have a read through the original paper published by Watson and Rayner, on their 'Little Albert' study:

- Watson, J. B. and Rayner, R. (1920). Conditioned Emotional Reactions. *Journal of Experimental Psychology,* **3**, pp. 1–14.

References

Brophy, J. (1997). *Motivating Students to Learn.* Guilford, CT: McGraw-Hill.

Gross, R. (2010). *Psychology: The Science of Mind and Behaviour.* London: Hodder Education.

Kohn, A. (2001). Five Reasons to Stop Saying 'Good Job'. *Young Children,* **56**, (5), pp. 24–28.

Maslow, A. H. (1943). A Theory of Human Motivation. *Psychological Review,* **50**, pp. 370–396.

Miller, G. A. (1962). *Psychology: The Science of Mental Life.* Harmondsworth: Penguin.

Pavlov, I. P. (1927). *Conditioned Reflexes: An Investigation of the Physiological Activity of the Cerebral Cortex.* Oxford: Oxford University Press.

Penn, H. (2008). *Understanding Early Childhood: Issues and Controversies*. Maidenhead: Open University Press.

Skinner, B. F. (1935). Two Types of Conditioned Reflex and a Pseudo Type. *Journal of General Psychology*, **12**, pp. 66–77.

Tapola, A. and Niemivirta, M. (2008). The Role of Achievement Goal Orientations in Students' Perceptions of and Preferences for Classroom Environment. *British Journal of Educational Psychology*, **78** (2), pp. 291–312.

Watson, J. B. and Rayner, R. (1920). Conditioned Emotional Reactions. *Journal of Experimental Psychology*, **3**, pp. 1–14.

Woolfolk, A., Hughes, M. and Walkup, V. (2008). *Psychology in Education*. Harlow: Pearson.

6

A sense of me

The psychological ideas in this chapter

- extroversion and introversion

- Big Five personality theories

- identity rather than personality

- internal 'self' and social 'self'

- self-esteem

- self-concept

- self-efficacy.

First things first

Who are you? Who am I? Who are the tutors who deliver their knowledge on education? What is it that makes people different from each other but at the same time have a 'sameness'? Which words might you use to describe yourself or a friend?

REFLECTION BOX 6.1   Understanding yourself first

Here are a number of words that we sometimes use to describe ourselves and other people.

moody	touchy	sociable	passive	careful
thoughtful	peaceful	rigid	restless	outgoing
carefree	active	controlled	quiet	reserved
excitable	impulsive	pessimistic	easy going	talkative
calm	honest	loud	strict	reliable

What we would like you to do for this activity is to pick out the ones that you feel describe you (make a note of them) and then to re-do the activity as if you were one of your friends. In other words, take a moment to look through the words and pick out the ones that you feel your friends would choose to use to describe you. Try to do this as *honestly* as you can!

Did you find that easy or a little difficult? Let's say you found that easy . . . does that mean you are '*easy-going*'? Or would it mean that I should stipulate that you must be '*intelligent*' because you found it easy? Or, putting it another way, does that mean I should state that you must be a '*hard-worker*' because you found it easy? Plus, if you actually completed the task, surely you should be described as '*keen*'?

According to the founding father of psychology, William James (1890), these questions are part of the core aspect of what psychology is all about. For example, a valuable *definition of psychology* has been provided by Gross (2010: 1) who states that it is '*the study of the mind and behaviour*'. Therefore, understanding who a person is (their mind) and how that can impact their behaviour are questions that the discipline of psychology have been grabbling with for the past century. As someone who aims to work, either with or, within an educational system, these are also important questions for you to grabble with, as you will ultimately be faced with interacting with hundreds of pupils or students over the course of any possible career route.

Defining a person

Where do we start, then? Going back to those words that I gave you to choose from earlier, which of them do you think may be *positive* words in relation to being a student? Which of them provide an idea about an attribute that means the person is more likely to be a '*good*' student? Which of them would highlight the possibility of a '*not so good*' pupil; or, in other words, a '*difficult*' student or a '*struggling*' student?

Take a moment to go through that list and see if you can highlight the words using different colours. Use one colour: for words that depict a positive student and another colour for words that depict a student in a more negative light. If you're not sure what a word is trying to 'say' then leave it uncoloured as we can come back to these afterwards.

The reason we have asked you to do this, is because the topic of personality, identity and the self have had a number of perspectives that have been applied to it from psychology. This means it can become a messy topic to research and understand for students. Hopefully, the activity of highlighting the words as *positive* or *negative* was also a little messy and difficult. For example, what did you think the word 'quiet' depicts? Some of you may have used the *positive* colour for this word. That is because you may have envisaged a '*quiet*' child as someone who is capable of listening and attending to a teacher. Or, you might have seen them as more likely to be thinking and considering the material that is being taught . . . and that is why they are '*quiet*'.

However, some of you may have used the '*negative*' colour for the same word. This is possibly due to a '*quiet*' child being depicted as someone who is not engaged with the learning tasks set. Furthermore, they may be more *unlikely* to ask for help, if they are generally a quiet person. Neither of these positive or negative ideas are wrong and neither of them are right! What you have just drawn upon to complete that task is called a '**discourse**'. These are sets of beliefs that human beings have developed over time about a certain topic that are collectively accepted as being '*factual*'. According to Benwell and Stokoe (2006) and Burr (2003), we use these all the time as they often enable us to make quick judgements about something, which hopefully then guides our behaviour or the expected behaviour of someone else.

For example, one discourse that is apparent within the UK is that upon entering a room for a job interview our behaviour is expected to follow the norm or rules of engagement relevant to the situation. For example, we generally say hello and shake one of the hands of all the individuals in the interview panel. This idea of how to enter an interview is not a *real rule*. The idea has developed, because human beings are social creatures and we love to chat about our experiences. Therefore, whenever we have been to an interview we have discussed how we entered the room. After a number of people have stated that they followed that pattern of behaviour and it got a good outcome (e.g. they got the job) a *discourse* has developed that indicates that this is the best option of entering the room if you want a good outcome!

Discourses can be useful for human beings, but at the same time they can also be restrictive and controlling. Take the hypothetical interview previously: what if this interview is for a children's entertainer position and the interviewers have made it very clear that they want someone who can '*think outside the box*' and be '*dramatic*'? In other words, they are looking for someone to come in and '*wow them*'! Along comes an individual who believes they are just that . . . they enter the room, jump up onto the table and then proceed to shake the heads of all the interviewers, rather than their hands! They have immediately broken the general social rules of engagement and muddled up the way that they have chosen to engage with the interview (in other words, they have attempted to '*think outside the box*' and be '*dramatic*'). However, they don't get the job because the interviewers had a different idea about what they meant by being '*dramatic*' and '*thinking outside the box*'. They had envisaged the personality or identity of that person to be different to how the interviewee had interpreted the job description.

This is the same problem with the discourse that surrounds the notion of who we are. In psychology we have two camps: one which believes we develop a **personality** (which is believed to be stable and consistent across time) and the other which believes that our notion of self is more of an **identity** (which is *malleable* and tends to change from situation to situation). Both of these ideas offer educationalists an important perspective that can be utilised within a classroom setting. The first one we will look at is personality.

Personality theories

Allport (1961: 28) once defined personality as 'the dynamic organisation *within* the individual of those psychophysical systems that determine his characteristic behaviour and thoughts'. I have italicised the word 'within' in that definition as that is what tends to make personality and identity theories different. One sees our characteristics as an internal process (personality), whereas the other sees it as more of a social process (identity).

At a basic level, personality theories (of which there are many!) *tend* to be firmly founded upon the premise that personality is *relatively fixed* from birth. Therefore, their ideas are based within the nature camp in the whole nature versus nurture argument. For example, Eysenck and Eysenck (1975), plus Eysenck by himself (1947, 1995), have published widely on his ideas and he originally came up with the notion of *extroversion* and *introversion*. Take a look at Table 6.1 to see what characteristics he envisaged an extrovert and introvert to develop.

TABLE 6.1 Showing Eysenck's expected characteristics for introverts and extroverts

Introvert	Extrovert
Quiet and retiring kind of person	Boisterous, fun-seeking individual
Prefers the company of a good book to the throes of a wild party	Very social, loves parties of group activities
Has a number of intimate friends but can be distant at times	Has numerous friendships but tends not to get too personal
Well-ordered and organised, tends to plan well in advance	Enjoys excitement so tends not to plan ahead as they enjoy the rush and hectic-ness of life
Takes life seriously, and keeps their feelings in check	Carefree and very easy-going, often reported to be optimistic but impulsive
Is seldom angry as they prefer to remain in control of themselves and situations	Can be aggressive and emotional which means people see them as unreliable and sometimes uncontrollable

Adapted from Gross (2010)

REFLECTION BOX 6.2   Reflection point

Read through the list of extrovert and introvert characteristics in Table 6.1 on extroverts and introverts. Whilst you are reading through each one, see if you can spot any of the words that you used earlier to describe yourself.

■   Are you more of an *extrovert* or an *introvert* according Eysenck?

Consider what this would mean in a classroom full of children.

■   How could you use this information to understand the type of activities that each pupil may prefer?

Eysenck's notion of extrovert and introvert has been linked with the successfulness of conditioning individuals' behaviour patterns (see Chapter 5 if you need to review what this is). For example, he claimed that introverts can be **easier** to condition than an extrovert and this is due to the biological make up of their nervous systems. Eysenck's main problem was that only half of the research that was carried out to test his hypothesis found support for his idea. However, his idea on conditioning was tested in various ways, including to see whether extroverts or introverts were more likely to suffer from depression, anxiety, schizophrenia and even drug addiction.

Psychologists have continued to study what they believe to be *personality traits* (e.g. Cattell 1965; Fiske 1949; Kline 1993) and when we bring all the main ideas together, we are faced with what is often called the *five-factor-model* or the **Big Five** (McCrae and Costa 1997; Gross 2010). This notion implies that there are five *universal* traits or strands that make up an individual's personality and which all function on a continuum basis (e.g. you may be sociable: but this can be broken done into *very* sociable, *somewhat* sociable and to the opposite end of *un*-sociable). Therefore, each trait contains expected characteristics (see Table 6.2 on p.77). However, some psychologists have criticised the use of a continuum design for personality characteristics, as they believe it adds to the very notion of having a '*normal*'/'*desirable*' and '*atypical*'/'*undesirable*' personality type. What do you think?

TABLE 6.2 Showing the five personality traits and the expected characteristics of each

Neuroticism	**Characteristics:** temperament, general anxiety control (anxious/calm), mood, and emotional stability (happy/sad)
Extroversion	**Characteristics:** sociability, excitability, assertiveness, aggressiveness and emotional expressiveness
Openness	**Characteristics:** imagination, intelligence, creativity, sophistication and insight
Agreeableness	**Characteristics:** trust, kindness, affection, altruism and pro-socialness
Conscientiousness	**Characteristics:** competence, reliability, thoughtfulness, organisation and mindfulness

However, in defence of this model, the reliability and validity of personality traits have been tested repeatedly and studies generally find positive results in relation to both of these evaluative measures (Chamorro-Premuzic 2007). However, some psychologists call into question these studies as they are often carried out within Westernised societies; therefore, they are often challenged for being *ethnocentric* (e.g. based on specific ethnic groups: usually 'white', middle-class Americans or Europeans). Additionally, Moghaddam (2002) argued this often means the findings are not generalisable to all humans as the research is often based on well-educated populations (e.g. centred on students within university departments). *If you would like to learn more about these criticisms in relation to personality theories, see the links and related literature signposted in the 'Extended Research Tasks' section at the end of this chapter.*

One of the problems with measuring the Big Five personality traits is that it is often carried out via questionnaires and psychometric tests. This means the participants are asked at one specific moment in time to think about who they are and how they might react to a certain situation. To demonstrate why this is not a particularly good way of asking individuals, have a go at the reflection activity in Reflection Box 6.3.

REFLECTION BOX 6.3   Reflection point

■ How are you feeling right now?

Have a think about the different traits and characteristics in Table 6.2 and try to pick out where you are **right now** on one of those continuums. Let's be honest, if you have been reading this book for the last hour . . . then you may be feeling *restless*, hopefully *thoughtful*, possibly a little *bored* and *distracted* by now!

Now, try and recall another moment in your life where you were doing the same activity but in a different situation. You may have been reading a book with a group of friends (possibly even the same book!). In that situation, you may have acted in the same way as above (*restless* after an hour of studying), again hopefully *thoughtful*, but would you have felt the same amount of *boredom* or *distraction*? Would you have been *bored* in that situation?

The only difference is the situation but this will draw out different responses from you. Hopefully, you were *happy* and *enthused*, *motivated* to get the studying done but at the same time *social* and *talkative*.

Hopefully, the last activity highlighted that, sometimes, we do similar activities but the situation and the environment around us changes the way we respond and the way we are represented. William James (1890) talked about this aspect when he declared that the 'self' has a *duality* to it. Consider what the personality trait psychologists have been attempting to do; their aim is to understand the internal aspects of who you are. But James (1890) believed that the internal aspect of the self was only one part of it. He stated that we have an 'I-self' and we have a 'me-self'. The I-self, is your internal perception of *who* you believe you are (what the personality trait questionnaires are attempting to measure). The me-self, however, is your social entity (the way people around you perceive you to be). However, James argued over a century ago that you cannot take the social self out of the inner self; they have to be considered together because each one of them interacts and impacts the other. That is why sometimes, within psychology, you come across the term **'identity'** (rather than 'personality').

Social construction of identity

When you step back and look at both aspects of the inner and social self, it is clear to see that each one could contribute to the **construction** of the other. For example, try to recall what your favourite lesson used to be at school. Now think about why it was your favourite. Was it because you were '*good*' at it? Was it because the teacher was '*good*' at teaching? Was it because it was *fun* and *enjoyable*? Was it the *room* that made the difference? The *memories* that it enabled (e.g. trips)? Was it the fact that your *best friend* was in that lesson so you *enjoyed* it more? Was it due to the *timing* that it took place at (e.g. last lesson of the week or just before lunch?). Was it a mixture of all of these possibilities? Last, did you change your mind about what your favourite subject was every month, week, day or even lesson?

The reason I ask this, is because one theory within psychology, called **social constructionism**, believes that the decision you made about which subject was your favourite did not come from an internal spot or personality trait/characteristic. Instead, it was a choice that was made due to your changing identity and social relationships. Burr (2003) argues that social constructionism believes that human beings focus on the interactions that we have with others and we use them to construct who we are. Therefore, your identity is made up of your inner preferences but also your social self and the *discourses* that surround any activities that you undertake. Remember, discourses are all around us in the form of language and artefacts (objects). It helps to form our 'common sense' thinking and can at times force us to act or become something that we don't want to become (Cartmell 2010).

For example, some children appear to love school, some appear to hate it and some don't show how they feel about it. Over time, discourses (common ways of thinking) have developed and are passed down through generations, either: in a written format or simply discussed with another person, and ultimately inform today's children how they are supposed to socially act. Let's take a stereotypical example of one child who enjoys school, one who believes they are good at learning and one who feels like they hate school. So the child who enjoys school will understand that they are *supposed* to be well behaved and act in accordance with the school rules. A child who believes they are 'good' at learning will feel like they are *supposed* to get most of the answers correct (because that is what is socially expected of them). A child who hates school will be informed through shared discourse that those who dislike school should act in accordance with a collective perspective: e.g. misbehaving, being difficult in class, not attending etc. The power of discourse (which includes stereotypes) should never be underestimated, but even more so when you are referring to children. This is because they are at a stage in their development where the social aspects of life become their main focus, which means discourses are especially potent for them (Doherty and Hughes 2014).

In relation to this point, human beings continually evaluate their surroundings and the reason we do this is linked to this idea of identity: we use it to build and evaluate our self-concepts, our self-esteem and our self-efficacy. This means, your identity is thought of as *flexible* and **malleable** and will often change according to any new information coming in (remember, this is in direct contrast to the ideas of the personality trait theories). To remain flexible, we are required to pay attention every second of every minute, observing, evaluating and reconstructing our identities in accordance to what is happening (or not happening) in the environment around us. Let's say those three hypothetical children discussed earlier have a different or unusual experience (e.g. respectively: not enjoying a lesson, getting a lower grade or actively enjoying a school day). Their interpretation of their environment is slightly different from before, during and after the event and this information will need to be self-evaluated to see if their identities or subsequent behaviour needs to be altered in some way.

Self-concept

This is a psychological term that is often confused, by students, with self-esteem. This is because it is similar, in that it requires us to constantly feed information into it so that we can evaluate who we are. However, it is not based on *affective* judgements like our self-esteem (discussed later in the chapter). Our *self-concept* is different in that it is more of a cognitive structure. Consider Piaget's (1970) ideas about our cognitive thinking processes; he argues that we attempt to build **schemas** all the time to help us map out the world within our brain. Our self-concept is the same type of process. It is similar, in a sense, to a filing cabinet that contains information on what makes the different aspects of who we are. For example, I (e.g. Cartmell) am a senior lecturer at a British university; I am also a mother and a wife. During my spare time, I work with the British Psychological Society and in particular with their Psychology of Education section. Each one of those sentences contained a number of terms that helped you to categorise me, which in turn provided you with information about who I am (e.g. lecturer, wife, mother etc.)! Within those categories, I could sub-divide them again (e.g. I may believe that I belong in the category of 'good mother', which is in the wider category of parent, or I might even decide that I am a fair to good kind of lecturer, which is within a wider category of teaching which is in the category education). The idea of the self-concept is that it continually changes due to the way our identity and experiences change.

This has direct relevance within a classroom, as learners continually alter their academic self-concepts based on how they appear to be working: in relation to their own self-imposed ideas and on the observations they make of others around them. For example, academic self-concepts are based upon subjects but they interact with non-academic content too. For example, a learner will generally have a category for school, which develops into individual categories for each subject studied (e.g. English, mathematics, science etc.). Within the English category will be concepts focussed on writing, reading and spelling. However, reading and writing concepts are also needed in science and mathematics! Furthermore, non-academic related concepts like personal relationships and friendships will be filed under a link to the 'school' concept. In other words, self-concepts are complicated but valuable tools that allow an individual to keep track of important information related to their changing identity.

Self-esteem

However, when we start to *evaluate* our actions or our worth then it is our *self-esteem* that we are using. Do you recall that I said I thought I could be classed as a fair-to-good lecturer earlier? If I am simply categorising myself for the sake of it, then it is my self-concept; but if I evaluate my performance based on evidence from something I have read or on what someone has told me, then it is my self-esteem that is making that judgement. Buckler and Castle (2014) argue that self-esteem should be thought of as a balancing act. Therefore, imagine, if you will, a see-saw! On one side of the see-saw is our understanding of our actual abilities and skills (our actual self). On the other end is what we want to be able to do (our ideal self). This acts as a platform for us to think about our learning goals and ideas and can provide motivation to achieve (see Chapter 5).

However, problems tend to arise when an individual sets their ideal self (e.g. appearance, abilities, skills or behaviour) much higher than the levels at which they currently value their present capabilities. Let me give you an example. My actual self (think of the see-saw again) believes that I am a fair-to-good lecturer. On the other end of the see-saw is my ideal self, which I have chosen to be an outstanding lecturer! Due to the fact that an outstanding lecturer is more valued by the society and profession that I live and work in, it will appear to reside in a higher position on my see-saw, compared to a fair-to-good lecturer (*which in true see-saw style:* has now been devalued, meaning it weighs heavily on one side of my see-saw). If I attempt to work at improving my teaching but don't seem to be re-balancing my see-saw then, according to Branden (1969), I will suffer from psychological pain. I may feel guilt and anxiety because I fear I am letting the students I teach, down. I may start to make comments or appraisals like '*That session could have gone much better, if I had worked at a much higher level then I just did*'. These might then progress to '*That session should have gone better but it couldn't have because I am only a fair lecturer, rather than an outstanding one*'.

These comments are extreme, but unfortunately it is quite easy for human beings to slip into a pattern that unfolds in this way. Making the changes to our behaviour or skills depends upon how much effort, time, persistence and motivation we invest in making them happen (Brophy 1997). I am sure you can recall at least one thing that you haven't been able to do straight away (after all, we are only human!) Did you keep trying to repeat the activity until you learnt how to do it? Did you invest lots of time and effort into it? Did you value gaining the skill over the amount of energy it would take you to achieve it? Did you seek out others who could model the behaviour to you? Were you excited about the opportunity to work on developing yourself or did you feel bored before you even began? An amalgamation of all of those factors is what comprising as our self-efficacy.

Self-efficacy

Bandura (1986) discussed *self-efficacy* as a measurement of our *belief* in our ability to work at and accomplish a task successfully. For example, he stated it was our '*beliefs in one's capabilities to organise and execute the courses of action required to produce given attainments*' (Bandura 1997: 3). Therefore, this is clearly different to our self-concept (categorising our actions, abilities and roles) and our self-esteem (our affective judgement of the worth of our actual and/or perceived actions or capabilities).

More importantly, research has shown that individuals with higher levels of self-efficacy tend to demonstrate increased motivation and interest and also greater persistence and perseverance than those with reportedly lower levels of self-efficacy (Brophy 1997; Kohn 2001). This means it is vitally important that we encourage children and young people to develop high levels of self-efficacy.

To do this, Bandura provided us with four areas of concern. The first, and strongest influence, is *personal experience*. This means providing a pupil with repeated opportunities to work on their skill or ability development. However, this *must* be done in a supportive manner, where the task is broken down into smaller details that will be well within the child's zone of proximal development (Vygotsky 1978). In relation to this is the second influence. Bandura believed that *vicarious experiences* would help to improve a child's self-efficacy levels and it can be used as a scaffolding technique (Bruner 1996). This means providing opportunities to pair up a child with a more knowledgeable 'other' who models the ability or skill required. However, they need to be successful in demonstrating this skill correctly, otherwise it can have negative impacts on the child who is observing.

Third, is the idea of *positive persuasion*. Bandura believed that using positive 'pep' talks that encourage and praise children for completing small steps of each task can really help their overall self-efficacy levels. This is because it helps them to envisage their goal more clearly and also helps them to feel more self-worth from each individual task. It is also a good idea to model this positive approach and challenge any self-defeating statements with encouragement. Finally, if the positive persuasive approach has worked, the child should feel physical and psychological *arousal*, which transfers into motivation (Brophy 1997). I am sure you will understand just how much difference there would be, if you felt engaged, excited and eager to start writing your next essay compared to anxious and worried.

REFLECTION POINT 6.4   Reflection point

■   What is your self-efficacy like?

Consider a task that you need to complete which you might not be looking forward to. Having read through this chapter:

–   what information can you take from it that you could apply to your own learning?

–   could you break the task down into smaller ones, meaning you could reward yourself when each one is achieved?

–   is there anyone else that could model the behaviour or task for you?

–   do you have a friend you could ask to give you a 'pep' talk? Or even better, try to give yourself one but remember the purpose – there should be no self-defeating comments within it!

■   What about your self-esteem?

The best way to improve your own self-efficacy is to make a conscious effort to only judge your own abilities and skills against themselves! Issues arise when we start to look at the marks or feedback that others around us have gained, especially if this causes us to gloss over the fact that our latest essay received a higher mark compared to the previous one! Read the feedback your lecturers provide, as we aim to highlight where you can improve but most importantly we also aim to highlight what you are doing really well with. Again, this can get 'lost in transition' if we remain fixated upon what grade we received and what that means in relation to everyone else's abilities.

To conclude, this chapter has looked at one of the most complicated areas of psychology: the *self*. It has put forward two main perspectives to what is meant by the term the 'self'. One is the personality trait theory which states that we are effectively born with certain characteristics, which means it can be difficult to change the way a person is. However, we have also looked at the social constructionist approach to the 'self', which believes we are continually constructing and reconstructing ourselves in relation to how we socially interact with our environments. From this, we looked at how our constructions of ourselves can impact our self-concepts, our self-esteems and our self-efficacy levels. Finally, it is important to take some time to consider all of this information in a little more detail, as it can be very useful when you are contemplating how to support an individual with their learning and its related goals.

EXTENDED RESEARCH TASKS

There are a number of books that will help to develop your psychological awareness of the 'self' identity and personality theories:

- Gross, R. (2010). *Psychology: The Science of Mind and Behaviour.* London: Hodder Education. (This is a good starting point for any education based student who wants to delve into psychological ideas further but wants an easy to read approach.)

Social constructionism

- Burr, V. (2003). *Social Constructionism.* London: Routledge.

Personality theories

Personality, individual differences and intelligence:

- McCrae, R. R. and Costa, P. T. (1997). Personality Trait Structure as a Human Universal. *American Psychologist,* **52**, pp. 509–516.

References

Allport, G. W. (1961). *Pattern and Growth in Personality*. New York: Holt, Rinehart & Winston.

Bandura, A. (1986). *Social Foundations of Thought and Action: A Social Cognitive Theory*. Englewood Cliffs, NJ: Prentice-Hall.

Bandura, A. (1997). *Self-Efficacy: The Exercise of Control*. New York: W.H. Freeman and Company.

Benwell, B. and Stokoe, E. (2006). *Discourse and Identity*. Edinburgh: Edinburgh University Press.

Branden, N. (1969). *The Psychology of Self-Esteem*. New York: Bantam.

Brophy, J. (1997). *Motivating Students to Learn*. Guilford, CT: McGraw-Hill.

Bruner, J. (1996). *Culture of Education*. Cambridge, MA: Harvard University Press.

Buckler, S. and Castle, P. (2014). *Psychology for Teachers*. London: Sage.

Burr, V. (2003). *Social Constructionism*. London: Routledge.

Cartmell, K. M. (2010). *Learning to Adapt to Formal Schooling: What are Children's Experiences of Their First Year?* Paper presented as part of a symposium at the BPS Psychology of Education Annual Conference, Milton Keynes: UK.

Cattell, R. B. (1965). *The Scientific Analysis of Personality*. Harmondsworth: Penguin.

Chamorro-Premuzic, T. (2007). *Personality and Individual Differences*. Chichester: John Wiley & Sons.

Doherty, J. and Hughes, M. (2014). *Child Development: Theory and Practice 0–11*. Harlow: Pearson.

Eysenck, H. (1947). *Dimensions of Personality*. New Brunswick, NJ: Kegan Paul, Trench, Trubner & Co.

Eysenck, H. (1995). *Genius: The Natural History of Creativity*. Cambridge: Cambridge University Press.

Eysenck, H. J. and Eysenck, S. B. G. (1975). *Manual of the Eysenck Personality Questionnaire*. London: Hodder & Stoughton.

Fiske, D. W. (1949). Consistency of the Factorial Structure of Personality Ratings from Different Sources. *Journal of Abnormal and Social Psychology*, **44**, pp. 329–344.

Gross, R. (2010). *Psychology: The Science of Mind and Behaviour*. London: Hodder Education.

James, W. (1890). *The Principles of Psychology: Vol 1 and 2*. New York: Henry Holt.

Kline, P. (1993). *Handbook of Psychological Testing*. London: Routledge.

Kohn, A. (2001). Five Reasons to Stop Saying 'Good Job'. *Young Children*, **56**, (5), pp. 24–28.

McCrae, R. R. and Costa, P. T. (1997). Personality Trait Structure as a Human Universal. *American Psychologist*, **52**, pp. 509–516.

Moghaddam, F. M. (2002). *The Individual and Society: A Cultural Integration*. New York: Worth.

Piaget, J. (1970). *Science of Education and the Psychology of the Child*. New York: Orion.

Vygotsky, L. S. (1978). *Mind in Society: The Development of Higher Psychological Processes*. Cambridge, MA: Harvard University Press.

7

Social or solitary learning

The psychological ideas in this chapter
■ innate learning theories: Piagetian ideas
■ socio-cultural theories: Vygotsky's and Bruner's ideas
■ learning styles.

Having looked at how the human brain develops and works in relation to thinking and cognition (covered in Chapters 2 and 3), and at how emotions, motivation and identity (covered in Chapters 4, 5 and 6) all influence a person's capacity to learn, this chapter returns again to the topic of learning. However, it attempts to discuss and evaluate the explanations proposed in relation to the *activity* of learning, because this is at the very centre of education itself!

REFLECTION BOX 7.1   Understanding yourself first

Consider how *you* learn best:

■ *Which activities appear to 'help' you learn better* (e.g. visually presenting key facts before an exam)?

■ *Do you prefer to learn in a particular way* (e.g. record lectures to listen to them later in place of frantically trying to write down everything said)?

■ After revising for an exam or test, can you recall the memorised information months and years later? If not, why not?

What is learning?

In Chapter 2, we explained that learning refers to the acquisition and use of new knowledge and skills. Don't worry, we didn't mislead you, but we did hold back some of the other definitions that have been put forward in relation to how learning may be viewed! That definition was chosen because it is widely accepted as a good 'all-round' definition and it helps to explain the basic concept of what makes up learning: *the acquisition of knowledge or skills*. However, there are other definitions and discussions that have been postulated over the years around what learning *is* or consists *of*.

For example, MacBlain (2014) drew upon a quote from Jarvis (2005) that essentially raised the question of whether learning takes place **within** a person or whether it only occurs as an **interpersonal** (external) concept. Therefore, Jarvis was querying whether learning should be considered as a *cognitive structure* or whether it is a *social and emotional experience*. This debate has raged for many years and we are still left with many questions concerning 'learning' that remain unanswered. One of the problems that researchers and academics face is that learning can never be held **constant.** Subjects and topics differ, teachers teach differently, learners are motivated differently, their life experiences are vastly different and their goals are of course different. This makes it increasingly difficult to measure and assess the notion of learning, as it is never usually the same from one day or experience to another.

Nature and nurture debate

Before we began to look at previous theories of learning, we wanted you to contemplate **why** we learn because we believe that this can have an impact on **how** you learn! Recall from Chapter 5, being **intrinsically motivated** is often more helpful when learning than being **extrinsically motivated** (Brophy 1997; Kohn 2001; Tapola and Niemivirta 2008). Now consider what this means, in relation to asking a pupil to learn how to write autobiographical text compared to an adult who genuinely wants to write an autobiography of their life. Although the skill to be learnt is the same, the motivation and overall goals are different.

In a controversial move, Howe (1980) once purported that learning is a **biological device** that functions to extend a human's capacity. This definition implies that learning is due to our genetic and physical/bodily structure; therefore, this fits quite neatly with an example of *learning to run*. The art of running has a biological or evolutionary based purpose. It is certainly needed if you are faced with a very dangerous situation that requires you to get out of harm's way very quickly! However, compare it to the art of drawing; does this have a biological basis to it? Drawing was used as an early form of communication many years ago and it is a skill that is delivered through the power of bodily movements. However, drawing and 'art' require some form of feedback from another human being. In other words, to communicate through drawing requires another person to look and digest the information and then to feedback on it (e.g. judging its quality or asking for a part of it to be reshaped or redrawn). Therefore, the *learning* of this 'skill' is a *social enterprise*. Imagine if there was only one human being on the planet – would communication through drawing be effective then?

Jarvis *et al.* (2003) have suggested that '*learning*' is not just about changing our behaviour (recall the 'behaviourist paradigm' in psychology) nor should we see it as a purely individualistic cognitive process that stems from the way the brain analyses incoming information. Instead, Cartmell (2010) has argued that it should be thought of as an amalgamation of all of the experiences that people have, with any learning that takes place being a representation of the individual's attempts at '*making sense*' of the said experiences. This eclectic definition has been made possible due to previous theories of learning 'paving the way' which is why it is important for education studies students to gain an awareness of the well-known theorists (e.g. Piaget, Vygotsky and Bruner) and what their ideas were regarding *what* and *how* learning takes place. To demonstrate these, this chapter will now present two contrasting arguments concerning learning.

Argument one – learning is an innately linked ability

In Chapter 2, we very briefly introduced you to the concept of *schemas*, first suggested by Piaget (1896–1980). Piaget argued that learning can only take place when a child has reached the required stage that would allow them to *cognitively* consider the proposed information (to be learnt). Therefore, Piaget put forward that learning is a cognitive or largely unseen internal process that has innate tendencies. Furthermore, he laid out a four stage theory of cognitive development which highlighted when and how children consider incoming information.

Stage one

Sensorimotor (0–2 years): The child uses lots of reflex actions to begin with until they start to develop some form of memory and inner thought capacity. This enables the child to use more goal-directed actions. They begin to understand that items still exist even though they disappear from view (object-permanence).

Stage two

Preoperational (2–7 years): The child is capable of developing a form of language that allows them to understand symbolic formations. This means that they can '*think*' through what actions they might need to take (use of cognition) or what action they have taken previously. However, they struggle to understand the perspective of another person and Piaget termed this notion as being ego-centric (e.g. self-absorbed!).

Stage three

Concrete operational (7–11 years): The child develops the ability to logically solve problems that are concrete based (e.g. tasks that use 'real' world items or problems). They are able to classify and conserve correctly (e.g. can order and sequence items according to size, or weight). They gain the ability to think from another perspective rather than just from their own (decentred) and can consider two or more perspectives at the same time.

Stage four

Formal operational (11–adult): This is the ultimate level of cognitive development and means a child can logically solve abstract problems (e.g. using imaginary concepts). Finally, they become much more scientific in their approach to thinking and analysing information.

These four stages estimate at what age a child is biologically capable of learning new skills or knowledge but it doesn't specify *how*. Yet, Piaget (1970) did postulate how this occurs, too. He argued that we inherit two tendencies: one is organising information through the use of ***schemas*** and the other is through ***adaptation*** to the environment (altering our thought processes because of an environmental impact).

Schemas

Schemas are the building blocks to our thinking capacity. Every time we come across an object or new piece of information, Piaget believed, we place it into a new hypothetical cognitive folder (*let's say we come across an unknown object*). This new folder will contain information about the item (*e.g. it's a living, breathing object*) that allows it to then be mapped onto another folder that shares similarities with the same information (*e.g. animals tend to be living and breathing objects*). The ability to map out our thinking processes internally allows us to make hypothetical connections with different pieces of information. Once this new folder has been created (it can be thought of as a 'filing cabinet' or as the memory drive of a computer) and connections are made, according to Piaget, we have hypothetically committed an act of self '*learning*'.

Adaptation

Adaptation is the other innate ability that Piaget stated we have. It involves the skill of adapting our thinking in response to the environment (it could be argued that this in itself is learning!). Two processes make up our ability to adapt and these are *'assimilation'* and *'accommodation'*. The first, *assimilation*, takes place every time we try to fit new information into an already existing schema. For example, when teaching children to add up a mathematical calculation, there are a number of ways of demonstrating '*how*' to do this. A child may already know and understand one specific way of adding 278 and 389 together, e.g. by writing the first number above the second and adding up the units, tens and hundreds one by one. However, if the teacher wants them to start calculating these bigger numbers cognitively (i.e. internally) they may show them how to estimate the totals first, e.g. add 280 and 390 then deduct 3. If the child has some comprehension of estimations and of adding and subtracting then, according to Piaget, they will assimilate this new way of calculating the answer. In other words, they will add the new information (e.g. new way of working out) into an already existing schema on mathematical calculations.

Accommodation

If the child had no other knowledge (schemas) on 'estimating totals', then they would need to *accommodate* this new piece of information. This means developing a new place or file (e.g. schemas) that they can use to contain this new information. Piaget argued that we tend to adjust our thinking when attempting to *accommodate* new information rather than adjusting the information to fit our way of thinking.

What Piaget meant by this adjustment was that we continually search for opportunities that will enable us to test our way of thinking to ensure that it is still valid and balanced. He called this process **equilibration**. In essence, this means that every time we receive a piece of information, we assess it and apply what we believe to be related or relevant schemas to it. If this enables us to understand the information then we remain balanced (e.g. we achieve **equilibration**). However, if none of the related or already existing schemas help us to fully understand the information we gain a sense of **disequilibrium** (e.g. our thinking, knowledge and behaviour becomes unbalanced). This results in us attempting to either *assimilate* or *accommodate* this new information until we achieve **equilibrium** again!

Importantly, as Woolfolk *et al.* (2008) noted, there are occasions when a learner may receive information that is too novel (e.g. a young child may overhear an older sibling carrying out an algebra calculation) and they can't apply *assimilation* or *accommodation* to it (e.g. the child has no knowledge or understanding that the alphabetical letter represents a missing number and can't comprehend this level of abstract thinking: *recall the four stages previously*). In this kind of situation, the learner chooses to ignore it so that they can return to the preferred *equilibrium* level. Therefore, it is important to understand that Piaget's ideas around thinking, cognition and learning are interlinked and have a *biological driver* at their helm. In other words, a child will be unable to process something that is *levelled above* the stage of cognitive development that they are 'biologically situated' at and they need to be able to build up their knowledge segment by segment so that they can remain balanced in their thinking by *assimilating* or *accommodating* new information.

REFLECTION BOX 7.2   Reflection point

Recall the four stages of cognitive development put forward by Piaget.

- Do you believe that **all** children move through each sequential stage?
- Can Piaget's stages be applied to different cultural groups of children?
- Can Piaget's theory explain **'gifted'** children?
- Therefore, can the theory accommodate those children who may be considered to be developing **atypically** in relation to their learning?

Piaget's theory has been heavily criticised for being based on *ethnocentric* ideals (Santrock 2008). Research has shown that the age ranges put forward were far too restrictive, as children can perform the noted activities well below the ages stated by Piaget (Hughes 1975; Das Gupta and Bryant 1988). However, it must be remembered that Piaget carried out his research in a time era where schooling wasn't nationally standardised across communities, and the children of today are much more likely to receive formal education much earlier and for longer (Penn 2008). *If you would like to learn more about the criticisms made against and the counter arguments concerning Piaget's work, see the links and related literature signposted in the 'Extended Research Tasks' section at the end of this chapter.*

Argument two – learning is socially orientated

Another theory, that education studies students are asked to evaluate, concerning learning comes from Lev Vygotsky (1896–1934). Often referred to as **sociocultural theory** or **social constructivism**, Vygotsky (1978) argued that the central component of learning stems from culturally-centred, social interactions. In other words, Vygotsky suggested that learning is a **social product** and not one that occurs solely *within* an individual. However, his theory does suggest that children develop internalised thinking/cognitive processes (Palincsar 1998) but it stresses that these only develop due to socially shared activities.

A now well-known concept of Vygotsky's is that any intended cognitive development must appear twice: at least once on a **social** level (*inter-psychologically*) and then on a **personal** level (*intra-psychologically*). Therefore, an activity might take place (e.g. learning to ride a bike) where the parent supports (or, as it is sometimes referred to, scaffolds) the child's learning by providing some instructions on how to peddle and steer. After a few trials and errors, the child will assimilate the information internally and is soon able to perform the same task without the parent's support. As Pritchard and Woollard (2010) suggested, it is this type of social interaction, dialogue and support that scaffolds this experience and learning for the child so that they can build up some form of confidence in relation to the task, which means they can then start to internally process the learning.

In connection, Vygotsky outlined a **Zone of Proximal Development** (often shortened to ZPD) in which he suggested that a child's thinking will often be found to be *just on the verge* of being able to solve problems by themselves. To enable them to understand it completely they need a little guidance, clue, or reminder from a **more knowledgeable other**. The idea is that children are capable of *valuable learning* at this point in their development if they *receive the social guidance needed* to reach the next level. If the guidance provided (e.g. support to problem solve or to learn a new skill) is far above their current level of development, then no amount of encouragement will enable them to reach that level. Furthermore, if a task is far too easy, because the child has already mastered the skill, they will become disengaged with the process of learning.

According to Vygotsky's theory, understanding a child's limits and current performance is vital. Just as important though, is building a classroom that comprises of a mixed ability *grouping* of learners, which allows for pupils to work with more knowledgeable others. Furthermore, a teacher must carefully listen and observe a child's learning journey so that they can balance out the tasks or learning provided with the knowledge of where the child currently is. Although assessment may be easier with older children (as they can be given tests or exams) it can be more difficult to carry out with younger children. However, Vygotsky's idea of *'self-talk'* can be useful for providing a window into a child's thinking processes (as discussed in Chapter 3).

One of the main criticisms of Vygotsky's ideas though is that he didn't provide enough information on how a child may process any incoming information (e.g. in the second step of learning: intra-psychologically). Although, it should be noted that Vygotsky unfortunately died at quite an early age (38 years of age) and therefore he didn't get the chance to fully develop his ideas (Kozulin 1990). *If you would like to learn more about Vygotsky's ideas on learning, see the links and related literature signposted in the 'Extended Research Tasks' section at the end of this chapter.*

There is so much more that could be discussed in relation to Piaget and Vygotsky's ideas, but to summarise them in relation to learning involves simply highlighting their specific but contrasting focus. In general terms, Piaget believed that learning was, first and foremost, an *innate ability which could be manipulated by environmental factors*. Conversely, Vygotsky advocated that learning was *predominately a socially constructed notion that then needs to be internalised*. They both understood the importance of internal and socially orientated factors when it came to learning but they tended to see each of these with differing levels of value.

Making sense of learning today

Considering today's fast-paced classroom and what drives it is now an important part of teacher training. What can Piaget and Vygotsky tell us about the delivery of materials to students? Take a look at the activity in Case Example 7.1.

CASE EXAMPLE 7.1

Below is a list of *'typical'* topics taught within an education studies course within the UK (hopefully, you will have learnt about some of them already!). After reading through them, consider the questions below and try to formulate an answer for each one.

National Curriculum Guidelines	Current Safeguarding Practices	
History of Education	Essay Writing	Research Techniques
Theories of Learning	Child Development	Observing Children

- Are the contents of this topic based largely upon learning historical or theoretical ideas? Or are they based upon learning practical skills?

- Does this topic require students to discuss and debate it to ensure they fully understand it?

- Is this topic more suited to memorising facts or formulae?

Hopefully, completing this exercise (Case Example 7.1) has allowed you to see that on a degree course, sometimes the content to be learnt may be delivered either from a practical or theoretical method. Remember, Piaget informed us that learners can think abstractly from 11 years old upwards, although there have been large amounts of research that have called into question the ages put forward and that have found children can demonstrate the skills much earlier than Piaget postulated, e.g. Hughes (1978). This means they could, potentially, be able to think about and *learn* theoretical ideas if they were simply delivered didactically (i.e. listening to them through a standard teacher-led lecture). Furthermore, Piaget's theory can be seen within the UK's National Curriculum as year groups are often segmented into Piaget's stages (e.g. transitions into Key Stage 1, 2, 3 and 4 are age related) and subjects are taught in line with the age ranges at which Piaget suggested that children are capable of learning specific skills. It is believed that this approach helps learners to build up schemas on individual topics so that information can be gradually be built up and assimilated.

Yet, what if the hypothetical 11 year old mentioned earlier was in fact 7 years old, and they were being asked to learn about the theory of relativity? This concept is generally quite abstract so, according to Piaget's ideas, this could cause a 7 year old some problems as they potentially wouldn't be '*cognitively developed*' enough to be able to learn this material. Does that mean we must stop teaching abstract ideas within primary schools? As we have highlighted all the way through this book, each child will be different and some children **can** consider abstract ideas at this age, but others may need it to be taught in a different manner or left unforced until maturation has occurred.

As you will recall, Vygotsky provided the **ZPD** idea which states that with some guidance from a *more knowledgeable other* (e.g. teacher, classroom assistant or more abled student) a child can be '*scaffolded*' to learn about complex topics if delivered through socially-oriented forms of activities. Within this example, the teacher could *teach* about the theory of relativity by being active (using lots of visual, and practical examples, e.g. using multiple senses) which would help the children '*see*' and understand the abstract ideas being put forward. Furthermore, being able to discuss and ask questions would allow the scaffolding to reach deeper into their cognitive processing than if they had to simply sit and listen.

In today's world, we are expecting children to start formal schooling much earlier than ever before, so we need to have an eclectic theory of learning that can explain what the best approaches are for teaching all ages of children. Jerome Bruner's (1915–present day) ideas on learning may help in this respect. Bruner (1996: 119) once stated that '*readiness . . . (to learn) . . . is not only born but made*'. This philosophical thinking led him to design his **spiral curriculum** theory, which suggests that a child should be given a variety of opportunities to learn the same piece of information (e.g. returning to learn and recall the same item a number of times). However, he believed that not only should the learning be built upwardly in small incremental movements based on raising the level of difficultly (i.e. in a spiral formation), but the general idea was that the material should be delivered in different ways to ensure the child could make *sense (e.g. process)* of it in a variety of ways.

Bruner believed in the notion of '**social pedagogy**', which holds that a child should be developed in an *holistic manner*, which means developing their academic abilities as well as their personal development (e.g. socially, emotionally and culturally). If this is achieved, he believed the child would then be able to make better *sense* of their world (*learning*) as they would have the **means** to consider the information from a variety of angles. This is a point that has been discussed at length, that **to learn** requires an approach or tool bag of skills that enables the information to be **processed more effectively**. This argument tends to be classified under the 'learning styles, dispositions and approaches' banner.

Approaches in learning

I am sure each of you will be able to recall a moment in your life where you have been struggling to 'learn' about something. You may have blamed the teacher (or lecturer) delivering the content, the other pupils or students in the room, the author of the book for writing it in a confusing manner, the fact that you were 'bored' or because you were not feeling very well. These are all common complaints given by learners who are not really sure why they haven't managed to grasp the learning set. However, a number of authors would argue that the main issue was possibly due to the approach (and motivation for) learning undertaken by the student. The most common term used for these are *'learning styles'*. Numerous authors have written about various versions; but, for this chapter, we will look more specifically at the style that is often considered to be the most helpful, which is **perceptual modality** types. As Bruner previously advocated, students' senses can dictate the way they process incoming information. Some students like to '*see*' information (visual), some like to '*hear*' it (auditory), some like to '*touch*' it (kinesthetic). Take a look at the following three tables (Tables 7.1, 7.2. and 7.3), which outline how each type/style of learner behaves in a standard lecture context and also what is recommended as useful revision techniques.

TABLE 7.1 Showing visually-based learners' characteristics and recommended techniques

Visually-based learner	
Lecture scenario	Tends to watch the actions of the lecturer or the props (e.g. PowerPoint)
	Enjoys watching video clips or animations.
	Can recall the actions of the speaker or the videos that were used
Recommended techniques	Seek out educational videos/films of revision topics
	Design colourful mind maps or essay plans

TABLE 7.2 Showing auditory-based learners' characteristics and recommended techniques

Auditory-based learner	
Lecture scenario	Tends to be attentive to the speakers
	Can recall spoken facts more easily
Recommended techniques	Record lectures and listen to them again as revision
	Read notes out loud, especially essay plans or notes

TABLE 7.3 Showing kinesthetically-based learners' characteristics and recommended techniques

Kinesthetically-based learner

Lecture scenario	Tends to be restless in lectures
	Can recall the actions that **they** have produced
	Enjoys being able to work with topics through touch and manipulation (e.g. acting, building models)
Recommended techniques	Turn any notes into a story that could be physically acted out
	Make abstract theories more practical by representing them using a concrete structure (e.g. a physical structure that could represent Vygotsky's ZPD)

Interestingly, it should be noted that most research has now highlighted that learners have **preferences** rather than absolute styles. This means it can be difficult for both teachers and children. For example, any teacher who believes in this approach will want to provide the information in as many ways as possible to ensure that all preferences can be met. This is not always easy (recall the examples previously where we considered teaching about the theory of relativity) and delivering the content in a visual, auditory and kinesthetic way will be, at times, extremely difficult and teachers will be restricted in the options available. This means that some children may find such sessions difficult to digest.

Franklin (2006) has suggested that these learning styles are unhelpful for teachers and children as they allow each of them to find a 'preference' which they want to stick with. If we are being honest, most of us will stick with something that we know works well rather than try to practise other skills that we find difficult. It is the *reliance* that we carve out that can then have a negative consequence on our learning later on; for example, when we are faced with a lecture that is didactic in delivery yet one of the individual learners has a kinesthetic learning preference. Therefore, it would be better if we develop skills in processing information in a holistic manner so that we can become the 'all-rounded' student that Bruner first proposed.

One other way of considering learning, which appears in all of the literature surrounding styles and dispositions of learning, is **surface** and **deep learning**. As Woolfolk *et al.* (2008) state, **surface** learning can be described as 'shallow', as it is concerned with *memorising facts* or *key ideas*. As the learning is focussed on a type of memorisation, the learning does not require deep or excessive links with other information and this restricts how securely the knowledge is then contained (see Chapter 3 for further information). This style of teaching and learning is passive and it is not held in our memories due to the lack of strong connections and it becomes lost very quickly (this explains why you forget information after the exam period!). Finally, it should be noted that learners often struggle to *see the relevance* of this type of learning and often require external motivational drivers (e.g. praise and certificates).

In contrast, **deep** learning is known to be a *heightened* sense of learning. In other words, it uses as many senses as possible, as each one helps to make a connection to another within the brain. The more connections that can be made in our memories, the more likely the information will remain there and will be retrievable later on. These additional layers of memory connections require organising and structuring, which is why the learning becomes deeply rooted within the brain and memory system. Furthermore, research has found that intrinsically motivated learners naturally take this approach, as they enjoy the challenge of learning about a topic and they are driven to hold onto that information for future usage (Kohn 2001).

But what does this mean in relation to teaching and learning? Learning has been theorised repeatedly by psychologists, educationalists and philosophers and the concept of learning has been defined in a variety of ways. Piaget believed learning is an innate ability that develops alongside a biological trajectory, but that it can be influenced by environmental impacts. Vygotsky, on the other hand, believed it was a truly social phenomenon, and it can only be initiated by first appearing in the social realm (and would then require internalisation afterwards). Last, Bruner argued that we need to ensure we allow and support children, from a young age, to be holistic learners, providing them with the skills and tools to make sense of the world around them. We shouldn't fall into the trap of developing specific ways of approaching teaching and learning activities; rather, educators should ensure that we differentiate learning sessions that allow for movement within the contextual shifts of life-long learning and personal development of all.

EXTENDED RESEARCH TASK

There are a number of books that will help to develop your psychological awareness of learning.

Good 'all round' books on learning

- Gray, C. and MacBlain, S. F. (2012). *Learning Theories in Childhood*. London: Sage.

- MacBlain, S. (2014). *How Children Learn*. London: Sage.

Piaget's theoretical ideas

- Piaget, J. (1970). *Science of Education and the Psychology of the Child*. New York: Orion. (One of Piaget's writings on his theoretical ideas.)

- Orlando, L. and Machado, A. (1996). In Defence of Piaget's theory: A Reply to 10 Common Criticisms. *Psychological Review*, **103**, pp. 143–164. (An interesting counter argument against the rising criticisms made of Piaget's work.)

Vygotsky's theoretical ideas

- Vygotsky, L. S. (1978). *Mind in Society: The Development of Higher Psychological Processes*. Cambridge, MA: Harvard University Press. (One of Vygotsky's seminal texts.)

- Kozulin, A. (1990). *Vygotsky's Psychology: A Biography of Ideas*. Cambridge, MA: Harvard University Press. (An interesting piece that covers the short life of Vygotsky.)

(continued)

(continued)

Bruner's theoretical ideas

■   Bruner, J. (1996). *Culture of Education*. Cambridge, MA: Harvard University Press. (One of Bruner's seminal texts.)

■   Smidt, S. (2011). *Introducing Bruner: A Guide for Practitioners and Students in Early Years Education*. London: Routledge. (A good introduction to Bruner's life and ideas.)

Learning styles

■   Woolfolk, A., Hughes, M. and Walkup, V. (2008). *Psychology in Education*. Harlow: Pearson. (This book provides much more detail on this aspect.)

References

Brophy, J. (1997). *Motivating Students to Learn*. Guilford, CT: McGraw-Hill.

Bruner, J. (1996). *Culture of Education*. Cambridge, MA: Harvard University Press.

Cartmell, K. M. (2010). *Learning to Adapt to Formal Schooling: What Are Children's Experiences of Their First Year?* Paper presented as part of a symposium at the BPS Psychology of Education Annual Conference, Milton Keynes: UK.

Das Gupta, P. and Bryant, P. E. (1988). Young Children's Causal Inferences. *Child Development*, **60**, pp. 1,138–1,146.

Franklin, S. (2006). VAKing out Learning Styles – Why the Notion of 'Learning Styles' is Unhelpful to Teachers. *Education 3–13*, **34**, pp. 81–87.

Howe, M. J. A. (1980). *The Psychology of Human Learning*. New York: Harper & Row.

Hughes , M. (1975). Egocentrism in Preschool Children. Unpublished doctoral dissertation. Edinburgh University.

Jarvis, P., Holford, J. and Griffin, C. (2003). *The Theory & Practice of Learning*. London: Routledge.

Kohn, A. (2001). Five Reasons to Stop Saying 'Good Job'. *Young Children*, **56** (5), pp. 24–28.

Kozulin, A. (1990). *Vygotsky's Psychology: A Biography of Ideas*. Cambridge, MA: Harvard University Press.

MacBlain, S. (2014). *How Children Learn*. London: Sage.

Palincsar, A. S. (1998). Social Constructivist Perspectives on Teaching and Learning. *Annual Review of Psychology*, **49**, pp. 345–375.

Penn, H. (2008). *Understanding Early Childhood: Issues and Controversies*. Maidenhead: Open University Press.

Piaget, J. (1970). *Science of Education and the Psychology of the Child*. New York: Orion.

Pritchard, A. and Woollard, J. (2010). *Psychology for the Classroom: Constructivism and Social Learning*. London: Routledge.

Santrock, J. W. (2008). *A Topical Approach to Life-Span Development*. New York: McGraw-Hill.

Tapola, A. and Niemivirta, M. (2008). The Role of Achievement Goal Orientations in Students' Perceptions of and Preferences for Classroom Environment. *British Journal of Educational Psychology*, **78** (2), pp. 291–312.

Vygotsky, L. S. (1978). *Mind in Society: The Development of Higher Psychological Processes*. Cambridge, MA: Harvard University Press.

Woolfolk, A., Hughes, M. and Walkup, V. (2008). *Psychology in Education*. Harlow: Pearson.

Researching psychological themes in education

The psychological ideas in this chapter
■ critical thinking skills
■ research paradigms
■ research methods
■ ethical considerations.

Research involving educational settings and support services has been surrounded by on-going arguments for many years now. Burton and Barlett (2009) have outlined one such argument, which called into question the *usefulness* of educational research. For example, they pointed out that some educationalists and policy makers believe that educational research is failing to support the *workers* within the education system. To evidence this, they recalled a lecture that was delivered by Hargreaves in 1996, in which he declared that funding should be removed from academics (e.g. university-based researchers) and placed firmly into the hands of educational practitioners (e.g. teachers and classroom-based support workers) so that they could carry out research. This helped to more firmly establish the notion of practitioner research, and even the Teacher Training Agency (TTA) got involved with the idea as they published their '*Teaching as a Research-based Profession*' document in the same year.

The TTA's acknowledgement helped to drive the *'study of education'* into being a research-based discipline. Therefore, in today's world, most education studies students are required to gain an awareness of what research comprises of, how to carry it out and how to critically evaluate it. Therefore, this chapter aims to help you understand the dominant research paradigms and the methods used within them. It will attempt to guide you through the process of choosing which research method is the most suitable option based on your research aims. And, last, it will seek to explain and prompt you to consider what critical analysis is and how it can be applied to published research. However, whilst every effort will be made to fully discuss all of these areas, as the topic of research methods is large and varied there will be a number of references that will need to be followed up by the reader if you want to overcome the complexities of research methodologies *(which can be followed via the links and related literature signposted in the 'Extended Research Tasks' section at the end if this chapter).*

REFLECTION BOX 8.1   Understanding yourself first

Consider what *you* already know about research:

■ Think back to some of the research that you have read as part of our studies so far. Do you agree or disagree with Hargreaves' argument that educational research is not helping workers within settings?

■ Who might be the most 'effective' researchers: practitioners or academics? What kind of skills and knowledge would each have compared to the other?

Critical thinking

The first area to consider, in relation to carrying out research as a student, is to understand what is meant by the term *'critical thinking'*. It is a notion that seems elusive to some students; but actually, if you have ever bought some food from a restaurant or a takeaway or even a pair of jeans from a shop before, then you have naturally been using your critical thinking skills! Take a look at Table 8.1, which attempts, in a light-hearted manner, to show you how you have already been analysing and evaluating the services of 'items'.

TABLE 8.1 What is critical thinking all about?

	Takeaway food	Jeans from shop	Academic research
Evaluating: ■ *The brand and makers* ■ *The product design*	■ *Well-known?* (What's the difference between Domino's and Pizza Hut?) ■ Does it look like it will be what you expected? (e.g. pizza and not a slice of bread with cheese on? ■ Is it made using similar methods and design? ■ Is the taste of it 'good' and likely to attract you back?	■ *Well-known?* (What's the difference between Levi's and ASDA's George brand?) ■ Do they look like they will last? ■ Do they appear to be made of the same material and methods as others? ■ Do they fit the way you want them to or would they suit someone else?	■ Early career researchers or well-known? (first publication or one of many?) ■ Does it explain and discuss what you expect it to? ■ Is the research carried out using similar methods to similar studies or has it been unique in its approach? ■ Does it use expected population samples?

Critical thinking is a skill that can be developed and there are various excellent study skills books available that go into more depth on how to develop this. In essence however, critical thinking means examining an idea and seeing whether it matches up to what you already believed about an item (e.g. Levi jeans have a snug fit but this makes them look great on – see Table 8.1) or provides another way of 'seeing' the topic/idea (e.g. Levi's 'snug' fit is an anomaly as they were never meant to fit in this way). Once you have gained an understanding of the alternative perspective, your next step is to evaluate the merit of the information (e.g. what is being *implied* with the revelation that Levi's jeans were never made to fit in this way? Are there connotations about body sizes, possible weight insinuations or manufacturing problems with body size generalisations?) What you do need to obtain, however, is an *objective* position (e.g. weigh up all sides of an argument and evaluate its strengths **and** weaknesses before making a judgement/evaluation). Therefore, referring back to the Levi example, were the insinuations that I proposed possibly provided in that way intentionally, or could it have been an emotional reaction, on my behalf, to the idea (e.g. most individuals become defensive whenever clothes and 'fitting' come into a conversation!)?

In a more academic manner, being able to critically evaluate academic research means paying attention to the focus of the research, the philosophy and discourse (e.g. this is the essence being portrayed so remember the Levi example of insinuations) provided by the research and also evaluating the methods and analysis of the data. Additionally, you can also look for and evaluate the research on its ethical design; as well as its consistency in using theories and theoretical ideas and how it applies these throughout. For example, is it mainly descriptive or does it use the theories to discuss and evaluate the data appropriately?

In summary, then, critical thinking skills entail actively seeking all sides of an argument, testing the soundness of the claims made and testing the soundness of the evidence used to support those claims. Having briefly highlighted a number of areas that can be critically considered in relation to academic research, this chapter will proceed to discussing the theory and practice behind each one in turn (e.g. philosophical approach, methods used and overall ethical design of research), so that you can start to understand both sides of the argument around any research ideas.

REFLECTION BOX 8.2   Reflection point

True or false?

- Critical thinking is a skill that is only used when carrying out research.
- I should use critical thinking to shine a light on the faults that can be found within an academic piece of writing.
- Critical thinking is being balanced and objective.

What is research?

Fraser *et al.* (2014: 35) explain the notion of research as a '*systematic pursuit of knowledge . . . a sceptical questioning of commonsense ideas . . . and a concern with empirical investigation*'. However, Evans and King (2006: 131) argue that it is '*not just about gathering information, it is also about analysing and interpreting that information and using it to make predictions or to build theories about the way the world works*'. Therefore, this means, in a very basic fashion, that it is similar to what you do when answering an essay question proposed by one of your lecturers. You **research** the information that you will need to analyse and evaluate the topic given.

REFLECTION BOX 8.3   Reflection point

From the list below, consider which potential research skills you already possess and make a note of the ones that you may need to develop:

■ developing focussed or detailed questions to guide your reading

■ searching the available literature to help you understand a concept or topic

■ making detailed notes of read literature

■ making a list of references used or bibliography of read literature

■ making connections between differing ideas or perspectives

■ using research literature as evidence to form or propose arguments.

According to Fraser *et al.* (2014) there is, however, one very clear difference that helps to define research, which is its reliance on **empirical investigation.** In essence, this is the investigation and subsequent collection of facts/data through *practical* and *scientific* methods (observations, interviews and questionnaires or experiments etc.), with the overall goal being to discover **new** information that can then be used to either: confirm or dispute previous knowledge. However, before a student can chose how to undertake a practical or scientific investigation, they need to consider which philosophical perspective of research fits with their intended research question or goal. These are often classified as the **positivist** and **interpretative** paradigms (a distinctive model of ideas or approaches).

First, the philosophy of the **positivist** approach is that research *must* be based on **scientific processes** that will enable **objective** (e.g. unbiased) data or conclusions to be drawn. Gross (2010) argues that this is the dominant research approach within the field of psychology, as the discipline is classified as a science subject and many psychologists therefore feel that psychological research should be carried out using similar methods to the other 'pure' science subjects such as chemistry and biology). It has been noted by Cartmell (2010) that this is often the preferred choice in educational research too, due to the political persuasion used when assigning research funding by government bodies.

This approach often has a **hypothesis** as its research question and its aim is that the data collected will help to support or disprove it. The analysis of collected data is therefore carried out in a statistical manner as this helps the research remain objective and value-free. It is often employed to answer **'what'** based research questions (e.g. *what* is the acceptable length of homework given to pupils?) Although, it should be noted that many research studies have also used this approach to answer '*how*' or '*why*' based questions, as they felt that an objective approach would be best overall. For example, let's say a researcher is interested in finding out why students spend specified amounts of time on their homework, a *why* question could be asked that provides a number of different responses that the participants are asked to tick – objectifying it through closed response questions (i.e. 2 hours allows time to think through activities). The ultimate goal of this paradigm is to design and collect data that represents unbiased, controlled information about groups of people or categorises of activities.

In contrast, the ***interpretative*** approach almost sits on the opposite end of a research continuum as it appreciates and seeks out the personal, emotive and value-based data that can be produced by human beings. Accordingly, this approach is interested in obtaining answers to **'why'** based questions as it seeks to ascertain how individuals make sense of the world around them. Therefore, as a social constructionist (*see Chapter 6 for more details*), Cartmell (2014) has argued that this paradigm aims to uncover the **essence** of social interactions and experience, allowing them to become known, unpicked and understood. Its findings are often displayed in creative ways (e.g. narratives or 'stories' or even films and 'art' forms) as the interpretation is subjectively analysed by the researcher.

This approach also holds, at its core, that the participants' voices are just as, if not more, important than the researcher when it comes to analysing and evaluating the research; therefore, they should be ***active partners*** in the full process. Ethically speaking, this means that this type of research often holds the '*rights of the child*' (UN 1989) at the centre of its design. Punch (2002) has argued that this means research involving children and young people can require extra vigilance and consideration when listening to their discursive voice. This means that the ethos and overall philosophy of the *interpretativist* approach aligns well to the **ethical guidelines** provided by the British Educational Research Association (BERA) and the British Psychological Society (BPS). Further discussion concerning ethical guidelines within research takes place later in this chapter, there is also an amalgamated and condensed version available in Table 8.3.

In summary, there are a number of pros and cons for both of these paradigms and these can be found in Table 8.2. These must be considered alongside the ***purpose*** of the research when choosing which approach is most suitable. Note, however, that sometimes the research aims don't automatically seem to fit with those two perspectives. For example, on first view, **action research** could be argued to be an approach in its own right but in general it tends to follow the ***interpretative*** philosophy. For example, according to Mac Naughton and Hughes (2009), its overall aim is to investigate and improve an aspect of ***professional practice***. Therefore, it is different to the positivist approach as it does not seek generalisable findings, although, the research itself could be designed to collect objective data! What is unique to this approach, though, is that it has a **'cyclical'** research process that involves (1) identifying an issue or area, (2) collecting data, (3) evaluating/ analysing the data, (4) planning an action that stems from the analysed data, (5) carrying out the action then (6) evaluating the action – finally returning, if needed to the first point of identifying if an issue (still) exists.

TABLE 8.2 Showing the characteristics of both the positivist and interpretative paradigms within research

	Positivist	Interpretative
Ontological assumptions (How the world exists)	■ One true reality that could be experienced in an identical manner	■ Reality is constructed and experienced individually – never experienced identically
Epistemological assumptions (*Acceptable/collectable knowledge*)	■ Only objective and factual information: generally represented as quantitative (numerical) data	■ Unique and personal accounts of experiences which display motives, meanings and reasons: general represented through qualitative data
Pros and cons	✓ Can generalise findings to wider population groups, objective data means limited risk of research bias ✗ Statistical information only shows the number of occurrences or categorises of answers – can't elaborate on the experiences of individuals	✓ Can understand unique situations or groups of individuals, subjective data provides rich and meaningful information ✗ Can't generalise its findings – can't make any recommendations for similar groups of individuals

Choosing a research method

Research methods are '*tools*' or '*ways*' of collecting data. Most of the currently used techniques will allow either quantitative data, qualitative data or a mixture of both to be collected.

■ *Quantitative* data is numerical – as in, you may want to count how many times a child passes the ball correctly or you may ask how old someone is in a questionnaire.

■ *Qualitative* data is very different as it is rich, personal and open-ended – as in, you may decide to observe how a child throws the ball and this means writing down every physical motion that you see but also noting down what was going on around the child at the same time (e.g. what type of room they were in, whether other children were present and what actions they were doing).

Some of you will have noticed that the descriptions of the two types of data are similar to some of the ideas followed in the *positivist* and *interpretativist* approaches. In general, they are – *positivists* collect *quantitative* data and *interpretativists* tend to collect *qualitative* data but they also collect *quantitative* data on occasions! Just try to remember that this approach is more flexible as to how data is used, whereas *positivism* allows no flexibility; all data **must** be *objective*.

Note of caution: many students often become confused when choosing which term/s to use when writing about research methods (e.g. **research methodologies** and **research methods**). Just as the definition of psychology means the '*study of the mind and behaviour*' (e.g. **psych** = mind and behaviour and **ology** = the study of), so too does the word *methodology* mean the '*study* *of methods'* (e.g. any word with the *'ology'* on the end means *'the study of'*). Therefore, don't fall into the trap of *'outlining the research methodology'* when writing your assignment reports! Instead, remember to use the term **research method** when you begin to highlight which one(s) you have chosen to collect your data through (e.g. experiment, interviews, observations etc.). The main techniques will be briefly outlined next – *however, if you would like to learn more about any of these methods, see the links and related literature signposted in the 'Extended Research Tasks' section at the end if this chapter.*

Experiments: These are generally considered to be a part of the *positivist's* camp as they test variables in relation to a *'cause and effect'* hypothesis (Gross 2010). Therefore, they attempt to isolate variables (as much as possible) from others so that the findings then indicate whether the tested variable *caused* or *influenced* the outcome. For example, providing one group of learners with a chocolate bar and one group with a piece of fruit before asking them to learn a standardised list of facts; then, testing each individual learner on how many facts they could recall. Counting *(quantitative data)* how many facts were remembered for each group would enable the researchers to see whether providing a chocolate-based or fruit-based treat would impact on a learner's ability to memorise facts.

Critical considerations: The main criticism of the experimental design method is that the findings only represent an **observable**, isolated segment of human life which is then manipulated in unrealistic and hypothetical surroundings or situations (Bronfenbrenner 1979). Therefore, it cannot claim to understand the cognitive thinking processes that human beings carry out as these are currently unmeasurable. In fact, some studies have asked participants to 'think out loud' in bids to ascertain what was being internally thought during the experiment. However, as human beings are social creatures, there is plenty of evidence to indicate that we often change our spoken language (e.g. tell a liar) in a bid to be seen in a positive light! This means that this method, although it is highly thought of in the science community, cannot remove or control the biases that humans inevitably bring with them.

Questionnaires *(also known as surveys)*: These are associated with the *positivist* approach, as they generally ask large numbers of questions that can be answered by ticking boxes or answering with specific responses (ages or height etc.). Their design is **scientific** and as **bias-free** as possible; therefore, there should be no *leading* or unclear questions used and to avoid this they are normally tested before the actual data collection is initiated. They often employ **'likert style'** questions which ask respondents to answer a question on a scale of 1–5 or 1–7 *(quantitative data)*.

e.g. How do you feel about attending after school detentions?

Please tick the appropriate box: ☐ 1 – dislike a lot ☐ 2 – dislike a little ☐ 3 – neither dislike or like ☐ 4 – like it a little ☐ 5 – like it a lot

Critical considerations: This method generally relies on asking participants questions about hypothetical situations or about their previous life experiences. The danger here is the implementation of a **blanket assumption** that everyone will understand the questions in the exact same way and that the answers given are '*correct*' and **mean the same as all the other responses** in the same category. As in the example question above, does ticking '4 – like it a little' mean the same 'thing' (emotion or thought process) as someone else who has ticked it? Using closed questions (e.g. pre-determined answers provided or questions that don't allow for additional information to be given) can be confusing and frustrating for responders (imagine if you sometimes 'liked' attending after school detentions but that depended on which teacher was monitoring them; but you never 'liked them a lot' – which response would you chose?) Being unable to ask questions about '*the questions*' (as surveys are often completed alone or away from the researcher) and the high time demands made on respondents means that this method struggles to achieve high return rates of questionnaires.

Interviews: These are definable as *conversations* between at least two people, with one person taking the role of interviewer, who asks the questions, and the other the role of interviewee, who answers the questions. It would be deemed a '*focus group*' if there were more than four individuals taking part at the same time. The interesting point about interviews is that they can collect quantitative or qualitative data. Furthermore, they can be **structured** (e.g. follow rigidly set time prompts, with every question being asked in the exact same way and order for every participant), **semi-structured** (e.g. interviewer follows prompts and question guides, but allows the conversation to develop where appropriate) or **un-structured** (e.g. conversation is focussed around a specific theme but questions can be asked '*in the moment*').

Critical considerations: This method can fall foul to what is known as the **researcher bias**. This is where the researcher (e.g. the interviewer) influences the interviewee; this can occur due to the way they ask the questions (e.g. tone of voice or the body language they display) or due to a perceived or real power imbalance between interviewer and interviewee (Sullivan and Riley 2012). Plus, it must be remembered that interviews tend to take place in a quiet, comfortable and convenient location which is usually outside of an individual's normal daily life pattern, meaning it lacks real-life representation. Taking a structured (and to a point, a semi-structured) approach can mean that the interviewer misses information that can help to explain the phenomena in more detail. Whereas, with unstructured interviews, the experience may become unmanageable with the discussion being 'off-focus' or it may struggle to move forward in a controlled manner.

Observations: These allow as much flexibility as interviews, as there are **structured observations** (e.g. observing only specific occurrences) or **unstructured observations** (e.g. noting down everything that the observers 'sees'). Within the structured observations approach, there are *event-sampling* techniques (e.g. using a tally chart to count how many times the observer notices the specific occurrence) or *time-sampling* techniques (e.g. only noting down what is occurring at specific time points: every 30 seconds or every ten minutes etc.).

Furthermore, as part of the observational method, there are **participant** and **non-participant** techniques. *Participant observations* involve the observer being a part of the activity or interaction being observed. They gain a deeper, richer insight into the process because they are a part of the process. Conversely, non-participant observers refrain from becoming involved (e.g. often standing at the back or side of the classroom in an attempt to restrain any impact their presence might have on the environment).

Critical considerations: These are similar to those from interviews, in that researcher bias (**observer bias**) can be difficult to overcome. Carrying out observations generally requires an individual to remain as emotionally detached as possible (unless they are a participant observer), in attempts to minimise any emotional responses which may influence *who*, *what*, *why* and *how* they observe and analyse the surroundings. Being a participant observer requires the researcher to 'become' a part of the situation, surroundings or experience so that they can write about what it feels like to be a part of it. This can place researchers in difficult situations that, at times, have meant that they had to choose between breaking the law and removing themselves from the research!

In summary, hopefully this brief introduction to the main techniques/methods available has allowed you to consider which of them may be most appropriate for your research question or aim(s). You may have also noticed that by using only one method you may be placing restrictions on the kind of data you can collect. Whilst it is generally acknowledged as best practice to **triangulate** (Denzin and Lincoln 2000) your data, which involves using at **least two different methods**, as an undergraduate student this is not always possible. Therefore, there is usually an expectation that students can discuss and demonstrate their knowledge and understanding of the different types of methods within research projects in place of carrying out triangulation.

CASE EXAMPLE 8.1

Consider each topic below and try to consider what kind of data could be collected in each example, according to the **positivist** and the **interpretativist** paradigm:

- documenting the *process* of learning mathematical calculations
- understanding the impact of play on self-awareness
- studying the metacognitions of 8-year-old boys
- investigating the starting school transition from parents' perspectives
- observe how 'differentiation' is employed within children's centre playgroup
- understanding the impact of animal-centred activities in pre-school settings.

Ethical considerations

Ethics can be defined as moral rules that regulate the way we think and approach research. In fact, whenever any psychology or educational researcher (including student researchers!) sets out to study any aspect of life they are bound by the **ethical code of practice** governed by either BERA or, for psychology-trained researchers, the BPS. Both organisations have outlined ethical considerations that *must* be adhered to at all times to ensure that researchers remain morally responsible individuals and to ensure the safety of those who have volunteered to be participants. To remain current, in an ever changing world, both sets of guidelines are regularly updated and *it is your responsibility* to ensure that you read the full guidelines set out by the relevant institution *before* you begin to collect any data. *If you would like to learn more about these two 'Learned Societies', see the links and related literature signposted in the 'Extended Research Tasks' section at the end if this chapter.*

Most degree courses now require students to submit ethical proposals of their research projects. So, you will need to design, ***ethically consider*** your research design and then re-design a number of times before you are able to put an ethics proposal forward without any hitches. (*N.B. this is quite normal for most researchers – both experienced and inexperienced!*) Your first consideration is whether the area or focus of interest may be deemed **'ethically unsound'**. In brief, this would involve any projects that involved breaking the law, causing physical or psychology harm to another (including animals), deceiving an individual or forcing someone to take part.

In Table 8.3 there is a mnemonic (which is a memory aid) that is useful for remembering the core aspects of ethical considerations. Have a read through the brief points made within the table, which are situated next to each core consideration. However, it is important to further discuss the added considerations of carrying out research with children and young people. For example, ***informed consent*** is important for all participants but this can feel like an impossible task with children, especially very young children. In fact, students often 'opt' for settling for '*gatekeeper*' (head teachers or class teachers) –

TABLE 8.3 Basically 'ethics' is all about what you *can do* and *can't do* with participants

Ethical considerations (mnemonic)

Can	**C**onsent	*Informed consent* means participants are made aware (*before* data collection) of what they will be doing, why and what will happen afterwards
Do	**D**ebrief	Explain what will happen to their individual data and who and how to contact the research team for the overall findings. Furthermore, provide sign posts for participants to support networks (if appropriate)
Can't	**C**onfidentiality	Participants should always be given anonymity, but if this is not possible from the start, explain clearly how the data will be collated and when and how anonymity will be used in research outputs
Do	**D**eception	Participants should *never* be deceived during research unless there are *exceptional* circumstances – even then it is unlikely an ethics committee would approve any deceptive projects
With	**W**ithdrawal	Participants have the right to withdraw from all or part of your study, at any point. It is important to ensure that children are reminded of this before every interaction is taken
Participants	**P**rotection from harm	Participants should remain in the same physical and psychological *state* that they enter the research in. There should be no opportunities for potential harm to occur: before, during or after

sometimes called **'loco parentis'** consent (which is a Latin term meaning '*in the place of parents*') because they believe it may be too difficult to gain true 'informed' consent from the children themselves. Schools are generally well organised places and sometimes offer to help students by providing this **blanket of consent** (usually where the research involves activities that would be deemed the same as those undertaken by the children in normal day to day school life).

However, students should resist (where possible) the temptation to stop at this point and they should continue to seek both parental and child consent. By not providing the children with the opportunity to give consent, they are inadvertently disregarding the children's rights and treating them as research '*objects*' rather than full participants. As an absolute minimum, students should always seek *assent* from children (which is any recognisable signal that the child consents) whenever they engage in research activities with them. For example, if, when observing children, you notice two in particular, you should ask if it is ok if you watch them for a minute and make some notes. Even very young children can provide *assent* in the form of saying 'no' or turning their backs on you so that you can't see what they are doing. In connection to this, it should be noted that there are a number of ethically aware approaches to researching with children that students may want to consider. For example, Clark and Moss (2001) proposed the **'mosaic approach'**, which concerns itself with using participatory methods that aim to allow the children to be the researchers and data collectors themselves!

In summary: having critically outlined the main philosophical approaches to research, and carried out a similar critical discussion concerning the various research methods available to students and ethical considerations that they need to make, it is time to draw this chapter to a close. However, it is almost impossible to say that one's knowledge and understanding of research is ever complete! Therefore, it was felt that directing you to continue your learning journey by reading some of the excellent upcoming references would help us close this chapter whilst paying homage to the popular saying, '*As one book closes, another is waiting to be opened!*'

EXTENDED RESEARCH TASK

There are a number of books that will help to develop your psychological awareness of research methods.

FOCUS ON CRITICAL THINKING

- Cottrell, S. (2011). *Critical Thinking Skills: Developing Effective Analysis and Argument.* Basingstoke: Palgrave Macmillan. (One of the most engaging texts available that goes through, in detail, how to develop critical thinking skills.)

(continued)

(continued)

FOCUS ON RESEARCH METHODS

■   Burton, D. and Barlett, S. (2009). *Key Issues for Education Researchers.* London: Sage. (An excellent and thorough introduction to research for Education Studies students.)

■   Clark, A., Flewitt, R., Hammersley, M. and Robb, M. (2014). *Understanding Research with Children and Young People.* Milton Keynes: Open University Press. (An excellent text that discusses various specific points concerning research that involves children and young people.)

FOCUS ON ETHICAL CONSIDERATIONS

■   Clark, A. and Moss, P. (2001). *Listening to Young Children: The Mosaic Approach.* London: National Children's Bureau. (Details how and why we should involve children within research – rather than as 'objects' of research.)

■   Punch, S. (2002). Research with Children: The Same or Different from Research with Adults. *Childhood*, **9** (3), pp. 321–341. (An interesting article on the ethical considerations of research involving children.)

■   The British Psychological Society (BPS) has produced a Code of Practice for researchers, which can be found at their website: www.bps.org.uk (accessed 15 April 2014).

■   The British Educational Research Association (BERA) also has lots of useful information concerning ethical awareness and considerations: www.bera.ac.uk (accessed 15 April 2014).

References

Bronfenbrenner, U. (1979). *The Ecology of Human Development: Experiments by Nature and Design.* Cambridge, MA: Harvard University Press.

Burton, D. and Barlett, S. (2009). *Key Issues for Education Researchers.* London: Sage.

Cartmell, K. M. (2010). *Learning to Adapt to Formal Schooling: What Are Children's Experiences of Their First Year?* Paper presented as part of a symposium at the BPS Psychology of Education Annual Conference, Milton Keynes: UK.

Cartmell, K. M. (2014). *Socially Constructing the 'Starting School' Transition: How and Why do Children and Families Use the Available Child Development Discourse?* Paper presented at the BPS Developmental Psychology Annual Conference, Amsterdam: Netherlands.

Clark, A. and Moss, P. (2001). *Listening to Young Children: The Mosaic Approach.* London: National Children's Bureau.

Denzin, N. K. and Lincoln, Y. (2000). *The Handbook of Qualitative Research.* Thousand Oaks, CA: Sage.

Evans, K. and King, D. (2006). *Studying Society: The Essentials.* London: Routledge.

Fraser, S., Flewitt, R. and Hammersley, M. (2014). What Is Research with Children and Young People? In A. Clark, R. Flewitt, M. Hammersley and M. Robb (Eds), *Understanding Research with Children and Young People*. Milton Keynes: Open University Press.

Gross, R. (2010). *Psychology: The Science of Mind and Behaviour*. London: Hodder Education.

Hargreaves, D. (1996). *Teaching as a Research Based Profession: Possibilities and Prospects*. The Teacher Training Agency Annual Lecture, Birmingham: UK.

Mac Naughton, G. and Hughes, P. (2009). *Doing Action Research in Early Childhood Studies*. Maidenhead: Open University Press.

Punch, S. (2002). Research with Children: The Same or Different from Research with Adults. *Childhood*, **9** (3), pp. 321–341.

Sullivan, C. and Riley, S. (2012). Planning and Ethics. In C. Sullivan, S. Gibson and S. Riley (Eds), *Doing Your Qualitative Psychology Project*. London: Sage.

Teacher Training Agency (TTA). (1996). *Teaching as a Research-based Profession*. (Prepared by the TTA and the Central Office of Information 3/96. TETR J036294JJ). London: The Teacher Training Agency Information Section.

United Nations (UN). (1989). *The United Nations Convention on the Rights of the Child*. Available online: http://www.ohchr.org/EN/ProfessionalInterest/Pages/CRC.aspx. Accessed on 24th April 2014.

References

Alexander, R., Armstrong, M., Flutter, J., Hargreaves, L., Harrison, D., Harlen, W., Hartley-Brewer, E., Kershner, R., MacBeath, J., Mayall, B., Northern, S., Pugh, G., Richards, C. and Utting, D. (Eds) (2009). *Children, Their World, Their Education: Final Report and Recommendations of the Cambridge Primary Review*. London: Routledge.

Allport, G. W. (1961). *Pattern and Growth in Personality*. New York: Holt, Rinehart & Winston.

Asselineau, R. (1999). *The Evolution of Walt Whitman*. Iowa City: The University of Iowa.

Atkinson, R. C. and Shiffrin, R. M. (1968). Human Memory: A Proposed System and its Control Processes. In K. W. Spence and J. T. Spence (Eds), *The Psychology of Learning and Motivation*. New York: Academic Press.

Baddeley, A. D. (1986). *Working Memory*. Oxford: Clarendon Press.

Baddeley, A. D. (1996). Exploring the Central Executive. *Quarterly Journal of Experimental Psychology*, **49**, pp. 5–28.

Baddeley, A. D. and Hitch, G. J. (1974). Working Memory. In G. H. Bower (Ed.), *The Psychology of Learning and Motivation: Advances in Research and Theory. Vol. VIII*. New York: Academic Press.

Bandura, A. (1986). *Social Foundations of Thought and Action: A Social Cognitive Theory*. Englewood Cliffs, NJ: Prentice-Hall.

Bandura, A. (1997). *Self-Efficacy: The Exercise of Control*. New York: W.H. Freeman and Company.

Baron-Cohen, S. (1995). *Autism: The Facts*. Oxford: Oxford University Press.

Baron-Cohen, S. and Cross, P. (1992). Reading the Eyes: Evidence for the Role of Perception in the Development of a Theory of Mind. *Mind and Language*, **6**, pp. 173–186.

Baron-Cohen, S. and Wheelwright, S. (2004). The Empathy Quotient: An Investigation of Adults with Asperger Syndrome or High Functioning Autism, and Normal Sex Differences. *Journal of Autism and Developmental Disorders*, **34** (2), pp. 163–175.

Baron-Cohen, S., Riviere, A., Cross, P., Fukushima, M., Bryant, C., Sotillo, M., Hadwin, J. and French, D. (1996). Reading the Mind in the Face: A Cross-Cultural and Developmental Study. *Visual Cognition*, **3**, pp. 39–59.

Barrett, M. (2006). 'Like Dynamite Going Off in My Ears': Using Autobiographical Accounts of Autism with Teaching Professionals. *Educational Psychology in Practice*, **22** (2), pp. 95–111.

Benwell, B. and Stokoe, E. (2006). *Discourse and Identity*. Edinburgh: Edinburgh University Press.

Bermudez, J. L. (2010). *Cognitive Science: An Introduction to the Science of the Mind*. Cambridge: Cambridge University Press.

Black, P. and Wiliam, D. (1990). *Inside the Black Box: Raising Standards through Classroom Assessment*. London: GL Assessment Limited.

Blakemore, S. and Frith, U. (2005). *The Learning Brain: Lessons for Education*. London: Blackwell.

Braisby, N. and Gellatly, A. (2005). *Cognitive Psychology*. Oxford: Oxford University Press.

Branden, N. (1969). *The Psychology of Self-Esteem*. New York: Bantam.

British Ability Scale (in particular, the BAS3) tool used by educational psychologists. Available online at www.gl-assessment.co.uk/products/bas3 (accessed 1 March 2014).

British Psychological Society (2008). The Development Of Literacy: Implications of Current Understanding for Applied Psychologists and Educationalists. *Educational and Child Psychology*, **25** (3).

Bronfenbrenner, U. (1979). *The Ecology of Human Development: Experiments by Nature and Design*. Cambridge, MA: Harvard University Press.

Brophy, J. (1997). *Motivating Students to Learn*. Guilford, CT: McGraw-Hill.

Bruner, J. (1990). *Acts of Meaning*. Cambridge, MA: Harvard University Press.

Bruner, J. (1996). *Culture of Education*. Cambridge, MA: Harvard University Press.

Buckler, S. and Castle, P. (2014). *Psychology for Teachers*. London: Sage.

Burr, V. (2003). *Social Constructionism*. London: Routledge.

Burton, D. and Barlett, S. (2009). *Key Issues for Education Researchers*. London: Sage.

Cartmell, K. M. (2010). *Learning to Adapt to Formal Schooling: What Are Children's Experiences of Their First Year?* Paper presented as part of a symposium at the BPS Psychology of Education Annual Conference, Milton Keynes: UK.

Cartmell, K. M. (2014). *Socially Constructing the 'Starting School' Transition: How and why do Children and Families Use the Available Child Development Discourse?* Paper presented at the BPS Developmental Psychology Annual Conference, Amsterdam: Netherlands.

Cassidy, S. (2004). Learning Styles: An Overview of Theories, Models, and Measures. *Educational Psychology*, **24** (4), pp. 419–444.

Cattell, R. B. (1965). *The Scientific Analysis of Personality*. Harmondsworth: Penguin.

Chamorro-Premuzic, T. (2007). *Personality and Individual Differences*. Chichester: John Wiley & Sons.

Chess, S. and Thomas, A. (1996). *Temperament Theory and Practice*. New York: Brunner/Mazel.

Coffield, F., Moseley, D., Hall, E. and Ecclestone, K. (2004). *Should we Be Using Learning Styles? What Research Has to Say to Practice*. London: Learning & Skills Research Centre.

Clark, A. and Moss, P. (2001). *Listening to Young Children: The Mosaic Approach*. London: National Children's Bureau.

Clark, A., Flewitt, R., Hammersley, M. and Robb, M. (2014). *Understanding Research with Children and Young People*. Milton Keynes: Open University Press.

Cottrell, S. (2011). *Critical Thinking Skills: Developing Effective Analysis and Argument*. Basingstoke: Palgrave Macmillan.

Crone, D. A. and Horner, R. H. (2003). *Building Positive Behavior Support Systems In Schools: Functional Behavioral Assessment*. New York: The Guilford Press.

Damasio, A. R. (1994). *Descartes' Error: Emotion, Reason, and the Human Brain.* New York: Grosset/ Putnam.

Darwin, C. (1872). *The Expression of the Emotions in Man and Animals.* London: John Murray.

Das Gupta, P. and Bryant, P. E. (1988). Young Children's Causal Inferences. *Child Development,* **60,** pp. 1,138–1,146.

Davis, M. A. (2009). Understanding the Relationship between Mood and Creativity: A Meta-Analysis. *Organisational Behaviour and Human Decision Processes,* **108,** pp. 25–38.

Denzin, N. K. and Lincoln, Y. (2000). *The Handbook of Qualitative Research.* Thousand Oaks, CA: Sage.

Department for Education (2011). *Developing Sustainable Arrangements for the Initial Training of Educational Psychologists (Final Report).* London: DfE. Available online at www.education.gov.uk/nctl/ careeropportunities/b00201184/educational-psychology (accessed 22 March 2014).

Doherty, J. and Hughes, M. (2014). *Child Development: Theory and Practice 0–11.* Harlow: Pearson.

Dorfberger, S., Adi-Japha, E. and Karni, A. (2007). *Reduced Susceptibility to Interference in the Consolidation of Motor Memory before Adolescence.* Open-access article (PloS One, 2, e240). Available online at www.plosone.org/article/info%3Adoi%2F10.1371%2Fjournal.pone.0000240 (accessed 4 February 2014).

Ekman, P. and Friesen, W. V. (1971). Constants across Cultures in the Face and Emotion. *Journal of Personality and Social Psychology,* **17,** pp. 124–129.

Ekman, P., Friesen, W. V. and Ellsworth, P. (1983). *Emotion in the Human Face: Guidelines for Research and an Integration of Findings.* Cambridge: Cambridge University Press.

Elder, L. (1997). Critical Thinking: The Key to Emotional Intelligence. *Journal of Developmental Psychology,* **21** (1), pp. 40–51.

Evans, K. and King, D. (2006). *Studying Society: The Essentials.* Oxford: Routledge.

Eysenck, H. (1947). *Dimensions of Personality.* New Brunswick, NJ: Kegan Paul, Trench, Trubner & Co.

Eysenck, H. (1995). *Genius: The Natural History of Creativity.* Cambridge: Cambridge University Press.

Eysenck, H. J. and Eysenck, S. B. G. (1975). *Manual of the Eysenck Personality Questionnaire.* London: Hodder & Stoughton.

Eysenck, M. (2004). Applied Clinical Psychology: Implications Of Cognitive Psychology for Clinical Psychology and Psychotherapy. *Journal of Clinical Psychology,* **60** (4), pp. 393–404.

Fendler, L. and Muzaffar, I. (2008) The History of the Bell Curve: Sorting and the Idea of Normal. *Educational Theory,* **58,** (1), 63–82. DOI: 10.1111/j.1741-5446.2007.0276.x.

Fernández-Berrocal, P. and Extremera, N. (2005). About Emotional Intelligence and Moral Decisions. *Behavioral and Brain Sciences,* **28,** pp. 548–549.

Field, F. (2010). *The Foundation Years: Preventing Poor Children Becoming Poor Adults (Independent Review on Poverty and Life Chances).* London: Cabinet Office.

Fiske, D. W. (1949). Consistency of the Factorial Structure of Personality Ratings from Different Sources. *Journal of Abnormal and Social Psychology,* **44,** pp. 329–344.

Flavell, J. H. (1979). Metacognition and Cognitive Monitoring: A New Area of Cognitive-Developmental Inquiry. *American Psychologist,* **34,** pp. 906–911.

Florida, R. (2014). *Rise of the Creative Class* (3rd Edition). New York: Basic Books.

Forgas, J. P. (1995). Mood and Judgment: The Affect Infusion Model (AIM). *Psychological Bulletin,* **117,** pp. 39–66.

Foster, J. (2013). *Surfing Realities: A Practical Guide to Understanding the Nature of Reality and How to Enhance Yours.* Bloomington: Balboa Press.

Franklin, S. (2006). VAKing out Learning Styles: Why the Notion of 'Learning Styles' Is Unhelpful to Teachers. *Education 3–13*, **34**, pp. 81–87.

Fraser, S., Flewitt, R. and Hammersley, M. (2014). What Is Research with Children and Young People? In A. Clark, R. Flewitt, M. Hammersley and M. Robb (Eds), *Understanding Research with Children and Young People*. Milton Keynes: Open University Press.

Gapin, J. and Etnier, J. L. (2001). The Relationship between Physical Activity and Executive Functioning Performance in Children with Attention Deficit/Hyperactivity Disorder. *Journal of Sport and Exercise Psychology*, **32**, pp. 753–763.

Garratt, D. D. and Forrester, G. (2012). *Education Policy Unravelled*. London: Continuum.

Gathercole, S. E. and Pickering, S. J. (2000). Working Memory Deficits in Children with Low Achievements in the National Curriculum at Seven Years of Age. *British Journal of Educational Psychology*, **70**, pp. 177–194.

Gathercole, E., Packiam Alloway, T., Willis, C. and Adams, A. M. (2006). Working Memory in Children with Reading Disabilities. *Journal of Experimental Child Psychology*, **93**, pp. 265–281.

Geary, D. C. (2005). Role of Cognitive Theory in the Study of Learning Disability in Mathematics. *Journal of Learning Disabilities*, **38**, pp. 305–307.

GL Assessments. (2014) *How Is BAS3 Organised*. Available online at http://www.gl-assessment.co.uk/products/british-ability-scales-third-edition/how-bas3-organised (accessed 1 March 2014).

Goleman, D. (1995). *Emotional Intelligence: Why it Can Matter More than IQ*. London: Bloomsbury Publishing.

Goswami, U. (2004). Neuroscience, Education and Special Education. *British Journal of Special Education*, **31** (4), pp. 15–183.

Goswami, U. (2005). The Brain in the Classroom? The State of the Art. *Developmental Science*, **8** (6), pp. 468–469.

Grandin, T. (1995). How People with Autism Think and Learn. In E. Schopler and G. Mesibov (Eds), *Learning and Cognition in Autism*. New York: Plenum Press.

Gray, C. and MacBlain, S. F. (2012). *Learning Theories in Childhood*. London: Sage.

Gross, R. (2010). *Psychology: The Science of Mind and Behaviour*. London: Hodder Education.

Haefner, K. (2011) *Evolution Of Information Processing Systems: An Interdisciplinary Approach for a New Understanding of Nature and Society* (2nd Edition). Berlin: Springer Publishing Company.

Hamre, B. K. and Pianta, R. C. (2001). Early Teacher-Child Relationships and the Trajectory of Children's School Outcomes through Eighth Grade. *Child Development*, **72** (2), pp. 625–638.

Hamre, B. K. and Pianta, R. C. (2005). Can Instructional and Emotional Support in the First-Grade Classroom Make a Difference for Children at Risk of School Failure? *Child Development*, **76** (5), pp. 949–967.

Hannon, P. (2003). Developmental Neuroscience: Implications for Early Childhood Intervention and Education. *Current Paediatrics*, **13**, pp. 58–63.

Hargreaves, D. (1996). *Teaching as a Research Based Profession: Possibilities and Prospects*. The Teacher Training Agency Annual Lecture, Birmingham: UK.

Howe, M. J. A. (1980). *The Psychology of Human Learning*. New York: Harper & Row.

Hughes, M. (1975). Egocentrism in Preschool Children. Unpublished doctoral dissertation. Edinburgh University.

Inhelder, B., De Caprona, D. and Cornu-Wells, A. (Eds) (2014) *Piaget Today (Psychology Revivals. 2nd Edition)*. Hove: Psychology Press.

Isen, A. M., Daubman, K. A. and Nowicki, G. P. (1987). Positive Affect Facilitates Creative Problem Solving. *Journal of Personality and Social Psychology*, **52**, pp. 1,122–1,131.

James, W. (1890). *The Principles of Psychology: Vols 1 and 2*. New York: Henry Holt.

Jarvis, P., Holford, J. and Griffin, C. (2003). *The Theory & Practice of Learning*. London: Routledge.

Jordan, R. and Powell, S. (1995*) Understand & Teach Children with Autism*. Chichester: John Wiley & Sons Limited.

Karatekin, C. (2004). A Test of the Integrity of the Components of Baddeley's Model of Working Memory in Attention-Deficit/Hyperactivity Disorder (ADHD). *Journal of Child Psychology and Psychiatry*, **45** (5), pp. 912–926.

King, M. L. (1963). *I Have A Dream*. Speech given on 28 August 1963 in United States: Washington, D.C. during the 'March on Washington'.

Kline, P. (1993). *Handbook of Psychological Testing*. London: Routledge.

Kohn, A. (2001). Five Reasons to Stop Saying 'Good Job'. *Young Children*, **56** (5), pp. 24–28.

Kozulin, A. (1990). *Vygotsky's Psychology: A Biography of Ideas*. Cambridge, MA: Harvard University Press.

Leather, C. V. and Henry, L. A. (1994). Working Memory Span and Phonological Awareness Tasks as Predictors of Early Reading Ability. *Journal of Experimental Child Psychology*, **58**, pp. 88–111.

Lyotard, J. (1984). *The Postmodern Condition: A Report on Knowledge*. Minneapolis: University of Minnesota Press.

MacBlain, S. (2014). *How Children Learn*. London: Sage.

McCrae, R. R. and Costa, P. T. (1997). Personality Trait Structure as a Human Universal. *American Psychologist*, **52**, pp. 509–516.

McLean, J. F. and Hitch, G. H. (1999). Working Memory Impairments in Children with Specific Mathematics Learning Difficulties. *Journal of Experimental Child Psychology*, **74**, pp. 240–260.

MacNaughton, G. and Hughes, P. (2009). *Doing Action Research in Early Childhood Studies*. Maidenhead: Open University Press.

Martin, C. (2003) Memorable Outlier. *Current Biology*, **23** (17), 731–733. DOI: 10.1016/j. cub.2013.08.027.

Maslow, A. H. (1943). A Theory of Human Motivation. *Psychological Review*, **50**, pp. 370–396.

Miller, G. A. (1956). The Magical Number 7 Plus or Minus 2: Some Limits on Our Capacity for Processing Information. *Psychology Review*, **63**, pp. 81–97.

Miller, G. A. (1962). *Psychology: The Science of Mental Life*. Harmondsworth: Penguin.

Moghaddam, F. M. (2002). *The Individual and Society: A Cultural Integration*. New York: Worth.

Newell, A. and Simon, H. A. (1972). *Human Problem Solving*. Englewood Cliffs, NJ: Prentice Hall.

Oberski, I. (2006). Learning to Think in Steiner-Waldorf Schools. *Journal of Cognitive Education and Psychology*, **5**, (3), pp. 336–349. DOI: 10.1891/194589506787382431,

Organisation for Economic Co-operation and Development (OECD) (2007). *Understanding the Brain: The Birth of a Learning Science*. Centre for Educational Research and Innovation.

Orlando, L. and Machado, A. (1996). In Defence of Piaget's Theory: A Reply to 10 Common Criticisms. *Psychological Review*, **103**, pp. 143–164.

O'Shea, M. (2005). *The Brain: A Very Short Introduction (Very Short Introductions Series)*. Oxford: Oxford University Press.

Ovenden-Hope, T. (2013). Rethinking Secondary Education: A Human-Centred Approach. *Journal of Education for Teaching: International Research and Pedagogy*, **39** (3), 348–350. DOI: 10.1080/02607476.2013.796734.

Palincsar, A. S. (1998). Social Constructivist Perspectives on Teaching and Learning. *Annual Review of Psychology*, **49**, pp. 345–375.

Passolunghi, M. C., Vercelloni, B. and Schadee, H. (2007). The Precursors of Mathematics Learning: Working Memory, Phonological Ability and Numerical Competence. *Cognitive Development*, **22**, pp. 165–184.

Pavlov, I. P. (1927). *Conditioned Reflexes: An Investigation of the Physiological Activity of the Cerebral Cortex*. Oxford: Oxford University Press.

Penn, H. (2008). *Understanding Early Childhood: Issues and Controversies*. Maidenhead: Open University Press.

Petzold, C. (2008) *The Annotated Turing: A Guided Tour through Alan Turing's Historic Paper on Computability and the Turing Machine*. Chichester: John Wiley & Sons Limited.

Piaget, J. (1970). *Science of Education and the Psychology of the Child*. New York: Orion.

Piaget, J. and Inhelder, B. (2000). *The Psychology of the Child* (2nd Edition). New York: Basic Books.

Pinker, S. (1997*). How The Mind Works*. London: Penguin.

Premack, D. and Woodruff, G. (1978). Does the Chimpanzee Have a Theory of Mind? *Behaviour and Brain Science*, **1**, pp. 515–526.

Pressley, M., Borkowski, J. G. and Schneider, W. (1987). Cognitive Strategies: Good Strategy Users Coordinate Metacognition and Knowledge. In R. Vasta, and G. Whitehurst (Eds), *Annals of Child Development*, **4**. Greenwich, CT: JAI Press.

Pritchard, A. and Woollard, J. (2010). *Psychology for the Classroom: Constructivism and Social Learning*. London: Routledge.

Punch, S. (2002). Research with Children: The Same or Different from Research with Adults. *Childhood*, **9** (3), pp. 321–341.

Repovs, G. and Baddeley, A. D. (2006). Multi-Component Model of Working Memory: Explorations in Experimental Cognitive Psychology. *Neuroscience Special Issue*, **139**, pp. 5–21.

Robinson, K. (2011). *Out of Our Minds: Learning to Be Creative* (2nd Edition). Chichester: Capstone Publishing Limited.

Rushton, S. and Larkin, E. (2001). Shaping The Learning Environment. Connecting Developmentally Appropriate Practice To Brain Research. *Early Childhood Education Journal*, **29** (1), pp. 25–33.

Rutter, M. and O'Connor, T. (2004). Are there Biological Programming Effects for Psychological Development? Findings from a Study of Romanian Adoptees. *Developmental Psychology*, **40** (1), pp. 81–94.

Santrock, J. W. (2008). *A Topical Approach to Life-Span Development*. New York City: McGraw-Hill.

Schunk, H. H., Pintrich, P. R. and Meece, J. L. (2013). *Motivation in Education: Theory, Research and Applications* (4th Edition). New York: Pearson.

Searle, J. R. (2004). *Mind: A Brief Introduction*. Oxford: Oxford University Press.

Siegler, R. S. and Alibali, M. W. (2005). *Children's Thinking* (4th Edition). Upper Saddle River, NJ: Prentice Hall.

Skinner, B. F. (1935). Two Types of Conditioned Reflex and a Pseudo Type. *Journal of General Psychology*, **12**, pp. 66–77.

Smidt, S. (2011). *Introducing Bruner: A Guide for Practitioners and Students in Early Years Education*. London: Routledge.

Stout, M. (2006). *The Sociopath Next Door*. New York: Broadway Books/Random House.

Sudheimer, K. D. (2009). The Effects of Cortisol on Emotion. A dissertation submitted for the degree of Doctor of Philosophy. The University of Michigan.

Sullivan, C. and Riley, S. (2012). Planning and Ethics. In C. Sullivan, S. Gibson and S. Riley (Eds), *Doing Your Qualitative Psychology Project*. London: Sage.

Swanson, H. L. and Beebe-Frankenberger, M. (2004). The Relationship between Working Memory and Mathematical Problem Solving in Children at Risk and not a Risk for Serious Math Difficulties. *Journal of Educational Psychology*, **96**, pp. 471–491.

Swinson, J. and Harrop, A. (2012). *Positive Psychology for Teachers*. London: Routledge.

Tapola, A. and Niemivirta, M. (2008). The Role of Achievement Goal Orientations in Students' Perceptions of and Preferences for Classroom Environment. *British Journal of Educational Psychology*, **78** (2), pp. 291–312.

Teacher Training Agency (TTA) (1996). *Teaching as a Research-Based Profession*. (Prepared by the TTA and the Central Office of Information 3/96. TETR J036294JJ). London: The Teacher Training Agency Information Section.

Turing, A. M. (1950). Computing Machinery and Intelligence. *Mind*, **49**, pp. 433–460.

United Nations (UN). (1989). *The United Nations Convention on the Rights of the Child*. Available online: http://www.ohchr.org/EN/ProfessionalInterest/Pages/CRC.aspx. Accessed on 24th April 2014.

Vernon, P. E. (1987). *Speed of Information Processing and Intelligence*. Norwood, NJ: Ablex.

Vygotsky, L. S. (1978). *Mind in Society: The Development of Higher Psychological Processes*. Cambridge, MA: Harvard University Press.

Vygotsky, L. (1986). *Thought and Language*. Cambridge: MA: MIT Press.

Watson, J. B. and Rayner, R. (1920). Conditioned Emotional Reactions. *Journal of Experimental Psychology*, **3**, pp. 1–14.

Wing, L. (1996). *The Autism Spectrum*. London: Constable.

Wilde, O. (1998). *Oscar Wilde's Wit and Wisdom: A Book of Quotations*. Mineola, NY: Dover Publications.

Woolfolk, A., Hughes, M. and Walkup, V. (2008). *Psychology in Education*. Essex: Pearson.

Zajonc, R. B. (1980). Feeling and Thinking: Preferences Need no Inferences. *American Psychologist*, **35** (2), pp. 151–175.

Index

Philosophy and Education

An introduction to key questions and themes

By Joanna Haynes, Ken Gale &

Melanie Parker

The authors consider the implications of educational trends and movements through a variety of philosophical lenses such as Marxism, utopianism, feminism and poststructuralism. The book explores enduring themes such as childhood and contemporary issues such as the teaching of critical thinking and philosophy in schools. Features include:

- a range of individual and group activities that invite questioning and discussion
- case studies and examples from a variety of formal and informal education settings and contexts
- reference to philosophically informed practices of research, reading, writing and teaching
- suggestions for further reading in philosophy and education overviews and - and key questions for each chapter

Drawing on readers' experiences of education, the book reveals the connections between philosophical ideas and educational policy and practice. Part of the Foundations in Education Studies series, this timely textbook is essential reading for students coming to the study of philosophy and education for the first time.

For more information and to order a copy visit
www.routledge.com/9780415536189

November 2014 | 166 pages
Pb: 978-0-415-53618-9

Available from all good bookshops

ROUTLEDGE

New From Routledge Education

Policy and Education
By Paul Adams

Written specifically for education studies students, this accessible text offers a clear introduction to education policy. It aims to help the reader understand what is meant by educational policy, how policy can be made and the main discourses that have driven education.

Capturing the essential aspects of educational policy over the last thirty years, the book provides an overview of political themes in education demonstrating how education policy has progressed and the effect this and politics have had on schools. It then covers key themes such as performance, choice and professionalism to show how education policy is constructed and implemented and how this has impacted on education in practice.

Features include:

- activities that can be undertaken individually or as a group to promote discussion
- annotated further reading lists;
- chapter overviews and summaries

Written as part of the Foundations in Education Studies series, this timely textbook is essential reading for students coming to the study of education policy for the first time.

For more information and to order a copy visit
www.routledge.com/9780415697583

November 2014 | 166 pages
Pb: 978-0-415-69758-3

Available from all good bookshops

New From Routledge Education

Research and Education

By Will Curtis, Mark Murphy & Sam Shields

Specifically written for undergraduate education studies students, the book guides you through the process of planning a research project, the different research methods available and how to carry out your research and write it up successfully. Highlighting the theoretical and methodological debates and discussing important ethical and practical considerations, the book is structured to help you tackle all the different aspects of your project from writing your literature review, designing a questionnaire and analysing your data to the final writing up.

Features include:

- extension tasks -- to introduce new material and encourage you to think critically
- case studies -- with information on important studies and examples of research that have utilised specific approaches
- practical advice and tips -- to help you relate the topics discussed to your own on-going project work
- annotated further reading lists -- providing you with an opportunity to access more detailed and specific resources.

For more information and to order a copy visit
www.routledge.com/9780415809597

November 2013 | 240 pages
Pb: 978-0-415-80959-7

Available from all good bookshops

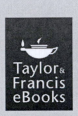

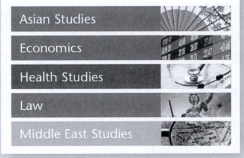